Advance Praise for *Another 20 Feet*

"What an amazing journey Aaron reveals in his book, *Another 20 Feet*. It is a path that everyone needs to take to find their purpose in life. I found myself reflecting on milestone circumstances in my own life that were similar to Aaron's. Even through disappointments, you can learn many lessons and grow as God shows Himself as real and 'an ever-present help in time of need.' If you are searching to find God's purpose for you, I believe you will have greater clarity as you read *Another 20 Feet*."
    – The Rev. Dr. Thomas J. Seppo,
        executive director, Operation Transformation

"*Another 20 Feet* is the perfect illustration of our need to see, sense, and engage God at a whole new level—regardless of our status in life. Whether your soul is parched and dry or filled to the brim and overflowing with the Holy Spirit, you'll enjoy Aaron's story of growth, connection, and the incredible closeness he discovers with God … simply by riding his bike. You'll walk away inspired and encouraged."
    – Scott Babin,
        lead pastor, BRIDGES Church,
        Port Huron, Mich.

"Our stories aren't perfect. They're simple, and messy, and beautiful. *Another 20 Feet* gives us the perspective we need to take each step with God. Be intentional, be still, and listen."
    – Karen Palka,
        founder and executive director, A Beautiful Me

Another 20 Feet

Through *tragedy, adventure,* and *triumph* –
one man's quest to understand God's role

AARON HULETT

Another 20 Feet

Through *tragedy, adventure,* and *triumph* –
one man's quest to understand God's role

ISBN: 978-0-578-65686-1 print
ISBN: 978-0-578-65687-8 ebook

Credits

Editing:	Positively Proofed
	info@positivelyproofed.com
Design, art direction, and production:	Melissa Farr, Back Porch Creative,
	info@backporchcreative.com

Table of Contents

Get the study guide!

Visit **ArcorFit.com/StudyGuide** and download a FREE companion study guide to follow along and get the most out of *Another 20 Feet*.

Introduction

Have you ever spent a lot of time and energy on something like growing a business, learning a sport or even studying to earn a degree, only to ultimately realize you were focusing on the wrong thing the whole time? What if there was a different way to live our lives? A way to live that gives us access to a compass of sorts, a compass to help guide our decisions, navigate our rough times, and keep us on course.

God has given me the passion and curiosity to pursue human performance, whether in the business world, mountain bike racing, or in life. He has allowed me to fail repeatedly, sometimes learn from my mistakes, and sometimes not. Our lives are the laboratory in which He molds, shapes, and hones us. That laboratory for me was my mountain bike. I have spent many hours on it in prayer, listening to an audiobook, song or podcast that He wanted me to absorb that day.

This book is a compilation of my journal notes from many of the lessons I learned from God while riding and many of the lessons He has taught me in all areas of life. I have discovered that He is my compass, becoming my ultimate guide and companion in my life's journey. It is also the story of trying things my way, then eventually learning the right way—God's way. Most importantly, it is a story of a relationship, a relationship with our Creator, one that's available to all of us.

We live in a time when much of the world seems to have Instant Gratification Syndrome. I call it "microwave mentality"; we want what we want and we want it right now! The very laws of nature go against all of this. When we learn to break out of that mindset, a whole new world opens up to us. The truth is, intellect comes from many hours of studying, building muscle comes from many hours of training in the gym, and building a lasting business comes from many weeks, months, and often years of successes and failures. The same is true for a relationship with our Creator.

The world teaches us to define our success or our dreams, then go after them with all we have. We are taught to work hard to get what we want. If you don't get it, just work harder. That sounds good, but it just isn't the truth in real life.

God has put on my heart why He created us and what He wants for us as His people. I believe that He wants us to live a truth-filled, joyful, and prosperous life—a life where He is at the center. God is at the center because we were created to run on His spirit. We need that connection with Him. We cannot run at our full potential without it. If not, there will always be something missing, something unfulfilled and incomplete.

My hope is this book will challenge you to take a step into His world; a world that allows you to see the unseen, a world that gives you the knowledge, peace, and contentment it has given me. For in Him, we live, move, and exist.

chapter one

What's It All About?

My Front Yard

I don't remember what day, month, or even year it was, but I do remember everything else in very clear detail. It didn't last long, but long enough for me to write about it now. I was somewhere around 10 years old and playing football in the front yard with my brothers, something we did often. I even remember exactly where I was standing in our yard at the time. The ball was accidentally thrown into the woods across the street. As I stood there waiting for one of my brothers to get it, I could feel something taking over my thoughts and emotions; a strong sense, a feeling of something present. It was a gentle and calming release of control. It felt as though time came to a standstill momentarily.

Strangely enough, I knew what it was, or should I say who it was. My initial reaction was confusion, but only for a split second. The gentle and calming release of control turned into a wave of peace that came over me. This was my first memory of encountering the living God's Holy Spirit. The entire encounter lasted about 10 seconds but left a significant impression on me, one that has lasted decades.

That day, I felt His presence say, "You will be a leader for me one day." A leader? At that age, I had no idea what this meant. Oddly enough, even as confused by this presence as I was, I knew without a doubt that it was God.

I had recently started attending a private Christian school; it was there, during quiet prayer time, that I began to experience His gentleness. I wasn't looking for a conversation with God that day. I just wanted to play football with my brothers, but He had other plans. For many years, I did not understand what that meant or how it really had anything to do with my life. I couldn't lie to myself; I knew something had happened, but I wouldn't see how it actually related to me for the next three decades.

In hindsight, I realize the Lord was planting a seed in me; a planting I completely forgot about within months. It withered and almost died for many years. But as with so many seeds that God sows throughout our lives, it eventually took root and is now growing into the life-giving plant He always wanted.

It's interesting how open a child is to the Holy Spirit. Children are malleable; they haven't had years of sludge poured into their hearts or heads. Possibly one of their greatest strengths, unknowingly, is that they are naive. As adults, we view being naive as a trait of weakness. Many people would say it's someone who can't think for themselves or someone who is just a follower. It can be a dangerous place to be, but in the right surroundings, it can be an amazing place to be. As adults, it's very hard for us to unlearn things. A child is a clean, blank slate in which an artist can begin their work. Of course, God knows this. He is the ultimate artist, after all. He created us!

North Hills

My exposure to Christianity as a young child meant occasionally attending church with my grandparents on Sundays. Together we attended the Riley Center United Methodist Church. My parents also sent my brothers and me to a private Christian school for half of fourth and all of fifth grade. We went to North Hills Nazarene, home of the Knights. This is where I met two people: Dan and Nancy Whitney. They possibly made the biggest impact on my life up to that point, second only to my parents. Mr. Whitney was a school administrator and Mrs. Whitney was my teacher. Attending school at North Hills was a unique experience for me. Our family had never been religious or what I call "churchy." Aside from Christmas and Easter, the only time we really attended church was for a wedding or a funeral.

At first my brothers and I were not happy about leaving our old school and our friends. But my mom and stepdad, Bob, had given us a pretty good sales pitch. They convinced us that it was going to be a good move. As kids, we didn't really have a say in such matters. Sometimes I think parents do this kind of stuff to make it easier on themselves. They probably just didn't want to hear us complain as much.

Their decision turned out to be an absolute blessing in my life. The seeds in my mind that were planted there eventually took root. Granted, it was many years later, and they almost withered and died many times, but they eventually took root. The Whitneys planted those seeds. They were unlike any other couple I had ever met or even knew existed up to that point in my life. They were a young, energetic couple. I would guess them to have been in their early 20s at that time. They lived differently than anyone else. I could sense this, even as a kid. It was almost as if they lived their life with love and compassion for others first, then everything else followed. I knew my parents cared for me, but I had never experienced an adult caring so much for others. At first it was somewhat foreign to me. As time went on, it became normal. My grandma used to say, "You are who you hang out with." I think in a small way I started to become like the Whitneys, realizing others could and should come first.

We only spent a year and a half at this school, but the things they taught us were lifelong lessons and truths I may have otherwise not been exposed to. They taught us about love—the true definition of love, not the watered-down version that always has strings attached. They taught us about Jesus and why He was so important. More importantly, they set an amazing example for all of us who attended there in how to live the right way. It was a sad day when they moved out of state to pursue what God had called them to do. I'm sure they went on to affect many more lives in such a positive way. I've often thought, "What if all teachers lived and taught that way?" Wow, imagine the impact on our world!

We left the Christian school in sixth grade, and that was it. Within a short time, I had forgotten much of what I had learned at North Hills. Since I never had any consistent exposure to faith, it wasn't a surprise that by high school I had become a borderline atheist. It was a gradual fade, not happening overnight, but slowly as life grew more difficult for me.

Early in high school, I began to be exposed to things that were new to me. I was big into the music scene, and there were activities that came along with that group of people—activities like parties, excessive drinking, and other bad influences. We didn't know it at the time, but the music we listened to heavily influenced us, too. Like many generations before and after us, we just wanted to rebel against our parents.

We would claim to be nonconformists. Looking back, I don't think any of us knew what we were truly not conforming to or rebelling against. Sure, there were some occasional social causes that sounded good to get behind, but I think we just didn't want to be told what to do. Our mindset was, "I want to do what's right for me. I want to do my own thing."

That mindset carried over into my spiritual life, too. When I say that I was a borderline atheist, I was 90 percent there, but a small part of me still had some doubt. It wasn't that I set out to or wanted to be atheist. I just couldn't rationalize how a supposedly loving God could allow such evil in the world. I also didn't see any proof that God was who He said He was. The truth is, I didn't see it because I wasn't looking in the right places. I was the type of person who needed proof or concrete evidence or I wasn't going to believe.

Even though part of my life was heading in the wrong direction, there were times when I couldn't get North Hills off my mind. Deep down, very deep down, buried below layers of confusion, doubt, and fear, I knew God was real and was who He said He was. I knew this because I had experienced the amazing warmth of His love through connection with Him as a child at North Hills. But at this point in my life, it was a faint, distant memory, barely recognizable anymore.

Figuring It All Out

As I got older, I would occasionally go to church, but it felt more like an obligation. It was not something I ever wanted to do or looked forward to. It was more like checking a task off of a daily To Do list. In hindsight, there was always a slight tug, occasionally gently pulling me toward God. I can't explain what it was, just an occasional small nudge. That nudge started to grow stronger as I hit my mid-20s.

I tried not to overthink it. I simply thought this whole religion, spiritual, God thing had to be dealt with. It bothered me that I was so unsettled in this part of my life. My simple logic was that eternity is a very long time. If my high school science teachers were right, we came from apes; therefore, I was basically just a collection of cells. I would die and fade away to dust—that's it, no more, nothing else, the end. I was okay with that. After all, I would be dead and I wouldn't have the ability to think any longer. So who cares, right?

But, on the other hand, what if Mrs. Whitney, my elementary school teacher at North Hills, was right? She taught me there was a God and He loved and cared for me. If I believed in His son, Jesus, I would have eternal life in heaven with God, the Creator of the universe. That's profound! At first it seemed like some crazy, far-out idea. I rationalized, "Who is this Jesus guy anyway and how can He issue me an eternal pass?"

The dilemma I could not get out of my mind for years was that if my science teachers were right, then there's nothing to worry about. I can live my life and do what I want. Ultimately, there would be no consequences for my actions, so what did it matter? It was all meaningless. If Mrs. Whitney was right, however, then I was in big trouble! There would be ultimate consequences for my actions or, in this case, inaction. I had to know the answer. This struggle for understanding began an intermittent, two-decade search for the truth.

For many years, I was on a happiness quest, not a truth quest. My logic toward God, evolution, and creation was flawed. Part of me just wanted to believe there was no God, evolution was how we came to be, end of story. It was hard to admit, but eventually I realized I wasn't being honest with myself. I was being hindered by the need to protect my accountability. In other words, I thought that if I believed in God, I would also have to accept His moral law. That would hold me accountable. I simply wasn't ready or willing to do that. It only changed when I began to seek the truth, not comfort or happiness.

It only changed when I began to seek
the truth, not comfort or happiness.

Seeking the truth is simple but not easy. I kept my mind open by looking into many different forms of spiritualism. My problem became who was right. Is it Buddha? Could it be the Muslims? How about Hinduism? What about the Jews? And, of course, then there were the Christians. Let's also not forget what I call the "universe bandwagon." This isn't necessarily a religion. It's more of a mindset stating that the universe is the ultimate guide, supplier, and overseer. Who or what is the universe? I didn't know which one was right, but I knew one thing: I believe in what I call absolute truth. That is, I know for a fact there are hard-and-fast rules that cannot be altered. Absolute truth is this: The apple is red and the orange is, well, it's orange. Honestly, I really felt like I was treating this whole thing like a menu in a restaurant. Pick your religion flavor today, this month, this year, etc. This wasn't good enough for me. I had to get to the bottom of it. If I was going to stake my life and, more importantly, eternity on it, I had to know the truth.

A Ship Tossed in the Seas

You could say researching different forms of spiritualism was an occasional hobby of mine. I didn't spend time on it consistently. If I saw a good book, an interesting TV show, or documentary, I would check it out. This is when I started reading the Bible a little more, too. Honestly, for a long time it just didn't make sense to me when I read it. I didn't really know where to start or what to read.

My mind was like a ship being tossed around at sea. One week I was a follower of Christ, then the next, I was unsure if it was just all in my head. The seeds of doubt had taken root in my mind for many years. The influence of culture, friends, and my overall surroundings directed my thinking. This seems to happen whether we want it to or not. In hindsight, I think I wanted to believe in God but didn't want to make the necessary changes in my life to walk with Him. It's so easy to justify anything if you want to.

The list of potential arguments against faith is long. Some people justify that believing in God isn't really what we think. The Bible was written by a bunch of people a thousand years ago, so it doesn't mean anything today. Others would say things out of ignorance like there's no proof that the Bible or God are real. Then there's the "hell argument." Some have tried to say that the church created hell as a way for religion to control people. I was never really driven by the fear of hell, though. I just truly couldn't identify with what that was. With all this confusion, it's no wonder we struggle so much.

Our science teachers didn't give us a choice, either. By the time I was in high school, it wasn't called the theory of evolution, it was just called evolution, and they almost never brought up creation. There are many other arguments against God, religion, or belief in Jesus, or whatever you want to call it. At one time or another, it seemed as though I bought into every single one of them over the years. It didn't change until I began my own search for the truth and stopped buying the lies I was told for so long.

The root of the problem with all of it was that I was taking someone else's word for truth. I just assumed because a friend, a role model, author, or scientist said it, it must be true. Let me say this very clearly to you right now: There is absolutely nothing more important in your life than the truth in this matter—not your job, not your possessions, not even your family. Nothing! Therefore, you have to go down the rabbit hole by yourself. No one can do it for you. As you read on, I hope you find guidance and comfort in your journey by learning from mine.

As my research continued, I realized there was simply too much evidence. I could clearly see atheism didn't hold up very well when put to the test. I realized that there was a mountain of evidence out there against the theory of evolution, too. I'm a person who needs things proven to me. Being the extremely logical thinker that I am, I need concrete evidence to believe something, not just old wives' tales, ideas, or opinions. The more I candidly looked at both sides, the evidence for a Creator by far seemed to outweigh the evidence for happenstance.

The more time I spent in prayer and reading the Bible, the more I could slowly begin to feel God's presence. The historical proof and evidence that Jesus was who He said He was and did what He said is overwhelming. I was starting to see the concrete physical evidence I thought I needed to see. What I didn't realize was that even though the physical, historical, and evidential proof was important, it was only one small piece of the equation. So many people stake the course of their thoughts on one thread or idea that they can't make sense of or overcome. This trap can falsely alter our direction in finding the truth. The matter of eternity is multifaceted. It's shortsighted of us to view it from such a narrow lens, yet that's exactly what I did for so many years. This applies to many areas of my life.

To be perfectly honest, I can't even wrap my mind around what eternity is. I just know that if I get to choose, I want to make sure I go to the right place. I started this journey thinking I may find some type of eternal pass to heaven. I ended up finding that's only one part of it. I would eventually find that the real power and fulfillment God offers could be brought to my life right now, today, if I choose.

Reading and understanding the Bible was my starting point. But this feeling, the feeling and knowing of His presence, was ultimately all the proof I needed. The more I pursued Him, the more He revealed himself to me. I could literally sense His warm, loving presence. This could not be fabricated. This was something outside of me, foreign to me, but I liked it. I innately knew it was good, warm, and peaceful, abundant with love and acceptance. I still had some doubts, but those seemed to fade slightly. It may sound strange, but a key part of growing in your faith can be doubt. Doubt is an ingredient that forces you to dig deeper.

It pushes you to uncover the truth. I was gradually and unknowingly learning to use this doubt as a tool to find the truth.

Doubt is an ingredient that
forces you to dig deeper.

Once you have experienced the joy of God and the loving forgiveness of Jesus, other ideas and religions will not matter. Every single one of them falls short of the fulfillment Jesus brings. Mankind is lured and tempted by the dark side. It's so deceptive that we can't even recognize it for what it is when it comes to us. Only through the power of a personal relationship with Jesus can you detect those influences. This is important to understand because even though we sometimes view sin (separation from God) as the main source of our struggles, it's not. That's only part of the battle. There are many forces at work that are constantly trying to pull us away from the truth. I firmly believe one of the devil's greatest tools is the confusion he creates with so many religions. It took me a long time and a lot of frustration before I figured that out. I often think of Ephesians 6:12 (NIV): *"For our struggle is not against flesh and blood, but against the rulers, against the authorities, against the powers of this dark world and against the spiritual forces of evil in the heavenly places."* I also find it interesting that many different religions can't seem to agree on who the real God is, but they all seem to agree on whom the devil is.

Lukewarm

As I continued my journey, I very slowly came to reestablish the relationship with God I had lost after leaving North Hills. However, at this point, I was what I call a "professional lukewarm Christian." This was not a semi-pro performance; I was a full-blown professional! You could even say I was on the All Star team. I was an expert at keeping God just far enough away from me so I could still live my life the way I wanted. I only wanted to change if it was my decision to do so. I had God right where I wanted Him, only calling on Him when I needed something or had a problem. You see, I had just enough experience with Him while going to church, reading the Bible, and praying to know that He was real and was who He said He was.

This state of detachment continued for a long time. Eventually, I couldn't deny it anymore. I could sense God's persistent yet gentle tugs to get my attention. For years I would dismiss it or ignore it. At first it was because I didn't necessarily know it was Him. At times, it was a feeling of conviction. I knew I was not doing the right things in life, but I did them anyway. Other times it was an overwhelming sense of knowing what I had to do but not having the nerve to do it.

Aside from those brief moments, my life was comfortable, or so I thought. It really wasn't, but it was comfortable to me because it was all I knew. Little did I know what amazing gifts waited for me! Despite what you may be thinking, I definitely do not have some unique gift or connection with God. What I am talking about is something every single one of us has the ability to experience. If you have the ability to read or hear the words in this book, you have the ability to have a personal relationship with God.

A turning point in finding truth for me was in understanding Scripture. The Bible says in John 14:6 (NIV): *"Jesus answered, 'I am the way and the truth and the life. No one comes to the Father except through me.'"* In other words, He is the gateway to God. His act of love toward us (dying on the cross) bridged the separation between God and man. That separation happened as a result of our (mankind's) decision to separate ourselves from God through our own free will. God is all about free will. He gives us complete freedom and control to do what we want and make our own decisions. We have the option to go through life with Him or without Him. With Him, the benefits far outweigh the fleeting, short-term benefits without Him.

As I grew more in my faith, things slowly began to change for the better. It was almost as if He was helping me change slowly, one layer at a time. At times he filled me with an overwhelming sense of peace and contentment. Other times, He challenged me and pushed me out of my comfort zone. It was unpleasant, but I knew it had to be done. In hindsight, I see that He was preparing me for another battle, one I had no idea was coming. I was in for a storm that would last several years and rock me to my very core.

"What About 'em?"

I was praying one day and really struggling with Jesus and how He fit in with other religions. I was at the point where I knew God was who He said He was. But I was still confused and more curious than anything else about all the other religions. How did He fit into them? Do all religions lead to one God? To me, this meant that despite what the world seems to teach, there had to be one truth and many were wrong. I always liked multiple-choice answers on tests in school. There was only one right answer to each question. Life can be and is this simple in many ways. I knew that if Jesus was whom He said and the Bible was in fact true, there was only one real God, and He is it!

When I really peeled the layers back and truly looked at each religion for what it is, they do not align with His message. I remember asking God in prayer a question I had asked Him many times before. He had never shown me the answer until this day. I said, "Lord, if you're real and who you say you are, what about all the other religions in this world?" This time He was about to give me an answer, one that I never would've expected and one that I could instantly and clearly feel.

There was absolutely no mistaking who or what it was. It was a swift and decisive answer. He said as clear as day to me, "What about 'em?" That was it. That's all He said. He didn't say it to me audibly. He said it directly to my soul. I could feel His answer. It was immediate, very loud, and very clear. I knew it did not come from me. Whatever doubt was resting in my spirit was removed that day and has never returned. It was not facts or logic that made this change inside of me. It was direct communication from our Creator.

Reading that answer in this book can be a little confusing. Your first thought may be, "What does 'What about 'em' mean?" Is he saying other religions may be true and not to worry about it? Was he saying they are not true? Or was He asking me what I thought? I can tell you assuredly, He only used three words, but what penetrated my heart that day was this: They are so insignificant that you and I aren't even going to waste another millisecond talking about or pondering them. Pay them no attention. Just keep your eyes and your focus right here on Me. The only way I can help you visualize this feeling is by sharing that He gave them the same significance that a lion who just came back from a successful hunt would give to a scurrying chipmunk. In hindsight, after I had time to let that experience sink in over the coming months, I realized something. God has seen these other religions come and go over the centuries. There have been hundreds of them, maybe more. Their significance to Him is nothing.

It can be foreign to think that God, the Creator of the universe, would ever be that personal with any of us. Encounters like that can easily be dismissed as chance to some. Others may say that only happens to certain people. I'm here to tell you that God wants a deep, personal relationship with every single person He has created. Yes, even you. I was trying to figure out the answer with logic, facts, and documented evidence. What I didn't know is the truth is often revealed in the unseen.

Whose Team Are You On?

Have you ever thought about whose team you're on? In our spiritual lives, we are on one team or the other. There is no neutral ground. Simply put, our lives are a collection of pieces that are actively building God's kingdom, or they are actively building the devil's kingdom. The things we do and say, the people we associate with, the habits in our lives that we give authority to, the lifestyle choices we make, all make up the outcome of who we really are. Some things are obvious; some are not. I ask you, whose team are you on? If you're not sure, ask the Lord to examine your heart and let Him in. Let Him reveal to you what you do not know about yourself. Then ask Him to come into your life and help you live it out. That way you can be sure you're on the right team.

Weird Churches, Weird Christians

I believe there's this big resistance or fear that many people have when it comes to going to church or even having anything to do with organized religion. It's almost as if people have this big chip on their shoulder about going there. For some, it's just an excuse not to go, while others have very legitimate reasons. I think many churches have alienated people over the years. For me, there is a long list of things that really bother me about organized religion.

Since I didn't grow up going to church much at all, I feel like I have a little bit of an outside perspective. When I started to go to church as an adult on my own, I didn't really know what to expect. To be honest, I was a little afraid to attend. I expected to find a bunch of hypocrites and people who were just going to tell me how bad I was and that I was going to hell—whatever and wherever that is. I had no idea. I just knew it was bad. I found most people were pretty cool. It turned out a lot of them were just like me. They were regular people who just wanted to learn more about this God thing. They were auto mechanics, accountants, the guy who cuts the grass for the city, and the lady who works at the corner grocery store. Most of them are regular, down-to-earth, good people.

At first, I checked out a few places. Every once in a while, at certain churches, I'd run into some of the weird ones. You know the ones I'm talking about. The ones who, outside of church, take pride in being abrasive about their religion and forcing it on others. Those people generally have 0 percent capacity to listen and 100 percent capacity to talk or be preachy. Then there are the ones who go over the top and use God as a tool to work out their own problems in life and project them on others. I can tell you this—most of those people in either category were probably weird before they became Christians. Adding knowledge about the Bible only changes their conversations. It doesn't change their lives from the inside. Only a direct and personal relationship with God does that.

The other weird ones, including pastors, use the Bible as a tool to separate us from God. In some denominations or types of churches, this is done with massive doses of fear and guilt. God has many roles: He is the Creator of love, peace, and kindness, but He is also the Creator of justice and truth. His role as a judge is often overplayed. Yes, he wants us to be like Jesus and strive to have no sin in our lives, but He already knows we can't live up to that. That's exactly why He gave us His son, Jesus. Jesus exchanged the very short-term pain of dying on the cross for eternal joy for us. His gift took that burden for us. In turn, our gift back to Him should be to continually improve and strive to live more like the example that He gave us in Jesus—more in love, kindness, and acceptance and less in fear, doubt, guilt, and shame.

So many people have been programmed to believe that God is mad at them and looking down on them with discontent. Yes, he wants us to live the right and pure way, the way that he has shown us in the Bible. He created us to live that way. The sad thing is, many have taken this role and exploited it into something it was never intended to be. If you're a parent, you correct your child when they do wrong, but you don't love them any less for their mistakes, do you? No, you correct them because you love them. God does the same for us. Our parents aren't perfect, but God is.

Another group of people who are weird are the ones who say one thing and do another—the hypocrites. The church isn't the only place filled with these kinds of people. They're even at my job, at the gym, and the grocery store. If we are to be perfectly honest with ourselves, this has been all of us at some point or another in our lives. We have all been hypocrites. Let's be real. Many of us have made the mistake of judging entire organizations on the actions of a one or two people. Right or wrong, it's human nature, and I guess that's what we do sometimes. I just want to say to you, don't let the actions of a few people determine your path or the direction of your life, especially your spiritual life. When we do that, we're essentially giving them authority over our lives. Don't give them that power over you.

I know a lot of people who say, "I don't need church. I pray and read my Bible at home." I think that's great, but I also think they're missing out on something very important. I could go on to many points here, but I'll just say this. Sometimes going to church isn't about you. Sometimes you just being there is what your friend or neighbor needs. They might need that hug from you today; they might need that smile or word of encouragement today. They may need something kind, warm, and loving in their life. They may not get it anywhere else. That's one aspect of church that we often overlook. It's about love—love for our Father, God, but also love for one another. This should be lived out in our everyday lives, and we can learn to do that at church. If your church isn't like that, maybe you need a new one. Hold up, though. Before you go off and start church hopping, sometimes the problem isn't our church. Sometimes it's us. Don't be afraid to face the truth.

chapter two

Pursuing a Dream ... My Way

Finding My Way

I've always been a hard worker. All through high school, I worked at the same pizza place. After high school, I attended community college for a year but realized school wasn't for me. I knew exactly what I wanted to do. I wanted to own my own business. This was not an accepted approach at the time. The established mindset was to go to high school, then go to college to get a good job. My thought was simple: I never plan on working for someone else, so why would I waste time and money going to college? Working with people came natural to me, and motivation was never a problem. Now I just needed to find the right business. The search led me to a few small projects, which opened doors to other opportunities. Finally, after a few years, I landed at a very small, relatively new mortgage company.

I was not self-employed like I wanted to be, but I found something that hit all my buttons. I was a 100-percent-commissioned employee. I could come and go when I wanted to. More importantly, I had the freedom to create. This position allowed me to create an income for my family. To do that, I created marketing campaigns to bring business in the door. In turn, I then had to create systems allowing me to deliver superior customer service and close real estate transactions efficiently.

This certainly did not happen overnight; it took many years. The two things I loved most about it were the challenge of putting it all together and working with people. It is especially gratifying in this capacity. It's an amazing day when someone buys their first home. I always thought it was pretty cool to be a part of that, and I still do.

The Green Book

As I crossed into my 30s, my motivation slowly began to shift to other areas. I loved what I was doing but felt limited. My thoughts turned to possibly owning my own mortgage company someday. The problem was, the company I worked for was phenomenal. The owners were good people and they built the business with integrity. In short, they made it easy for me to stay put. By nature, I am a very loyal person and just didn't believe that leaving was the right thing for me to do. My rationale was that as long as they ran the business this well, I would stay. However, I didn't want to be unprepared if that were to ever change. That's how the Green Book was born.

The Green Book is my collection of proven things that work in the mortgage industry, such as marketing, hiring, employee training systems, and more. I was never afraid to invest in something new, hire personal assistants, or try things out (for example, a new way to market my services or a new, more efficient way to get clients' loans closed). Some of those ideas didn't work out, but many of them did. Every time I found something that worked, the idea would go in the Green Book, a green, legal-size binder. I would write things down on yellow, legal-size paper and file them in this expandable folder, which grew quite sizable over the next five years. As the folder grew, so did my aspirations to bring it to reality.

The Decision

In my mid-30s, the company I was working for hit some growing pains. Things were going okay there, but recent changes pushed me to believe the time was coming to strike out on my own. Around the same time, I was introduced to a competitor at another company. We became friends and stayed in touch. One day he called and asked me to lunch. Both my reputation as a hard worker and my clientele had grown considerably over the years, and he knew it. I knew what the lunch was going to be about. He was looking to recruit me. He was very well respected in the community, so I went just to see what he had to say. This sort of thing happens often in our industry. People move from company to company looking for the bigger, better deal. I really had no interest in going to work for anyone else. I knew I would only make a move if ownership and, more importantly, input on the direction of the company were involved. I knew what I wanted, and I knew what things needed to be executed to build the company.

Failure is a critical part
of success.

Our meeting went very well that day. I realized he and I had a lot in common, shared the same values, and were looking to grow a business. Our initial meeting led to a couple more soon afterward. He was not only looking for a partner to help grow the company, but he also was looking for someone to help structure and organize that growth. This was the area I had been preparing for over the past five years. In truth, it was what I had been dreaming and thinking about since high school. Over that time frame, I had read many books and attended dozens of seminars on sales, time management, leadership, and more. Most importantly, through trial and error, I was applying what I learned every day. I have found failure is a critical part of success. As a matter of fact, I don't believe you're truly successful in any endeavor until you have experienced the seasoning of failure.

Now was the time to make the move, but I was still torn. There was the concern of financial risk, but that took a backseat to my loyalty to my current employer. I worked there for more than 10 years; they were my friends now. I knew I would eventually become a direct competitor, and that bothered me the most. I'm not sure if I would have actually made the decision to move forward if it weren't for what happened next.

The gentleman I had been meeting with could sense my hesitation. One day at a meeting, we were talking about the possibility of me joining them. He paused and asked point blank, "Are you in?" I'm honestly not sure where it came from, but I immediately responded with a "yes, I'm in." He then looked me in the eye, shook my hand, and said, "I'm trusting that you are a man of your word. This handshake represents that trust. This is a big step on both of our parts. By shaking my hand, you are confirming that we are doing this and there is no backing out from this point forward." We shook hands and it was confirmed. As I walked out of his office, I could feel many emotions overtake me. It was real. I had made the decision, and there was no backing out now. At that moment, I was nervous, excited, and scared at the same time. I literally almost threw up in the parking lot when I got to my car.

I had been praying about this decision. Unfortunately, this was a time in my life when I only used God as needed or when things weren't going the way I wanted. I hadn't yet learned and understood what a true relationship with Him looked like. My prayers were more like statements telling Him what I was going to do and that I needed His support. That is completely opposite of how He wants us to do things.

Everything else in this endeavor seemed to be a perfect fit. In my mind, I felt almost as if it were some sort of destiny. However, I was missing the most important part of the decision: God's presence and His unfiltered guidance. Somehow I could sense this missing ingredient, but I consciously ignored it. I justified that everything else was such a good fit. It had to be the right move. In truth, my mind was made up and I didn't want God's input.

In truth, my mind was made up
and I didn't want God's input.

A New Venture

We hit the ground running full speed, immediately implementing and then executing our game plan. Things went very well the first year. We had a few setbacks, but we were right on target with the plans we had made. It's amazing when you think about doing something for so long and then finally do it. It seemed almost surreal.

The newfound challenge had me exactly where I wanted to be. I loved having the autonomy to do whatever I wanted in my own company. I liked it because I knew the sky was the limit. If I built it, then I would be the one getting the rewards. At the same time, I was excited for our employees. We really wanted to build a place where people could come to work and have fun but be productive and do well financially, too. Things really seemed to be on the right track. However, in my zeal to get this company going, I rarely consulted God about any decisions. At that point in my life, I just wasn't as close to Him. Honestly, I didn't know what being close to Him even looked like. I would pray occasionally, but my prayers were really self-centered requests as opposed to actual open and honest prayers.

The company was doing even better going into our second year. By this time, we had expanded to a second location. We were strategically hiring and training new staff. Things were looking even better than our first year. The Green Book, my dreams of self-employment, and financial freedom all seemed to be coming together. Halfway through our second year, we signed a lease for a third location and hired more staff. Sales were good, it seemed, as if everything was falling into place.

That's when things started to change. I live in Michigan and the economy here is heavily tied to the automotive industry. All of the major auto manufacturers are located within about a 60-mile radius of Detroit. Even more suppliers from all over the state support the major auto companies. I live about an hour north of Detroit. A very large part of my local community was made up of many of these second- and third-tier auto industry suppliers, everything from seat belts to axles to door mirrors—you name it. Those suppliers do well when the industry does well, and they do poorly when the auto industry does not do well.

That meant our mortgage company was indirectly tied to the auto and housing industries. At the time, the economy was beginning to slow down considerably. Companies in almost every industry began to lay people off. Many companies just skipped the layoffs and outright let people go. That in turn affected auto sales. As the auto industry began to shrink, so did the housing industry. Within months, the domino effect was in full swing. On top of that, the housing industry had many problems right underneath the surface, which catapulted it from a downturn to a full-on national crisis.

I was all in, completely vested, and stuck right in the middle. Our company, the Green Book, my life's savings, and everything I had worked for through the years were falling apart. Within eight months, I lost it all. The worst part? There was absolutely nothing I could do about it.

chapter three

The Downfall

Dismantled and Broken

It happened so fast I almost didn't have time to react. The despair, anxiety, grief, and frustration were on a level I had never experienced.

It was absolutely the lowest point in my life. The worst part was that I could see no way out. The pride I once had was completely dismantled and broken. My normally very optimistic personality was fading quickly. When a life-changing event like this happens, you go through several phases. The first one is shock. This is when you say, "I can't believe this is happening to me." It's almost a state of denial. I have always been a fighter, someone who never gives up, and someone who always sees the glass as half full. As my new reality set in, I began to feel like a shell of a person. The fight was gone and I had nothing left, or so I thought.

When life brings you to your knees and keeps you down for a long time, you start to see things from a different perspective—one you couldn't possibly see when things are going well. I began to spend more time in prayer and I started to go to church more. This went on for almost three years. It was long and painful, but the work God did on me during that time could not have been accomplished any other way. One of the things I had to learn to deal with at the time was my anxiety. I came to realize anxiety was simply disguised fear—nothing more, nothing less. The problem with that is, you can't hear God in fear. In hindsight, the greatest tragedies in my life have almost always turned into the greatest lessons, and then eventually the greatest blessings.

You can't hear God in fear.

My Kitchen Table

I had good days and bad days, but there was one I'll never forget. I remember the day as though it were yesterday. It didn't start out as one of the good ones. I woke up that morning with the burden of a lifetime weighing on me. The frustration and despair were heavy on my heart, so much so that I was in an almost paralyzed state of mind. I didn't want to get out of bed, but I did. As I mindlessly dragged myself downstairs to the kitchen, I could feel my despair slowly turn to frustration. My only thought was, "Why me, God? What have I done to bring such destruction to my life?"

I have never been a stubborn person—persistent but not stubborn. That morning something clicked inside of me, something I hadn't given into in the past. While eating breakfast, I prayed and talked to God. In my frustration, I said, "Lord, I refuse to move from this table until you tell me what's going on." In my mind, I needed an answer and wasn't leaving until I got one. I was set. I dug in for the battle. The despair was at such a point that I was prepared to be there all day if needed. I closed my eyes, rested my head on the table, and cleared my mind. I waited motionless for 20 minutes, then 30 minutes, then 40 minutes. Head down, still motionless. The thought of moving, giving up, or giving in never even crossed my mind. I simply wasn't leaving until I got what I came for. Finally, the clock hit the 45-minute mark, and that's when it happened.

I could hear a small, faint voice in my head. It was saying one word over and over. It started out barely detectable, but it slowly grew louder and louder. Once I recognized what it was, I immediately realized it was not a word I wanted any part of. I tried to fight it and push it out of my mind. This didn't come from me. The message was coming from another source. It quickly grew louder and louder in my head. This word overtook me. It completely consumed any chance I had of dismissing it. It was simple but very powerful. The word was "gratitude."

Instantly the word became visual in my head. It started with one image, then another, then another. Suddenly they were coming at me so fast that I almost couldn't process them quickly enough. It was like watching a scene from a movie, one where the river dam gets a small crack. That crack turns into a larger one, then suddenly it breaks wide open and water gushes everywhere. That's exactly what was happening in my mind.

The images were of the things I had in my life to be grateful for: my children, my health, my wife, my immediate and extended family, my relationship with God, and so on. The images included even the smallest gifts He provides for us. It all happened in an instant, and it was completely overwhelming. There is only one response to this kind of event. I just sat there and wept. I was overcome with a mixture of emotions: gratitude, joy, love, and then sorrow for doubting God.

He didn't give me the answer I thought I was looking for that day. He gave me something better. God gave me hope. It's amazing when things are put into perspective. Our loving Creator knows what we need more than we do, especially at times when we can't see through our own self-interest, grief, or despair.

The Lord put one simple thought on my heart that day, a thought I have carried with me for many years since. I have fallen back on that lesson many times and will continue do so. In hindsight, I realize what a selfish and narrow viewpoint I had that morning. I sat there to defy God, to test Him, and get the answers I thought I needed, the ones I thought I deserved.

From Bad to Worse

Even in the toughest times, life continues on. I had been working as hard as I could to keep food on the table and the lights on. That included taking on any extra work I could find. I didn't tell a lot of people what we were going through, mainly just close friends and family. I was embarrassed about it, but soon the whole community would know.

One of the things I had been working at was a communications business with my friend Scott. We were looking for others to help us expand it. Friends of his, a couple named George and Lee, fit the bill perfectly. They had owned a very successful construction company and were well connected in the area. As soon as I met them, I liked them immediately. I can't say I had ever met more genuine people than those two. At first, I didn't know how to take them. I knew there was something different about them right away. They were genuine, loving, and caring people. It was almost as if they thought and lived differently than the rest of the world. In a way, they kind of reminded me of the Whitneys. They also had been going through some serious struggles with the downturn of the economy. But they were still so strong, calm, and never changed or compromised their character under such distress. What did they know that I didn't? It didn't take long to find out. They both had an amazingly close relationship with God, one that I couldn't possibly understand at first.

As I got to know them better, I began to see. They both came from very different backgrounds. George grew up in the gang life as a kid in Detroit. Lee was a complete atheist at one point in her early adulthood. Through a series of events in each of their lives, they both eventually came to know Jesus. God had given them the gift of adversity. It was that seasoning in life that gave them the wisdom and character to become the individuals they are. They were like a ray of sunshine breaking through the clouds in my life. I had no idea that someone could live this way. Lee had the closest relationship with God I had ever seen. She radiated the love of Jesus in her life. Anyone who knew her couldn't deny it. That sunshine was one of the few things that gave me a small glimmer of hope. It's amazing how God brings us the right people at the right time in our lives.

God had given them the gift of adversity.
It was that seasoning in life that gave
them the wisdom and character to
become the individuals they are.

Life was tough. The struggles were very real. It was not easy, but sometimes I would try to look at the positives, too. Our kids were doing well and we still had our health. However, we were starting to lose all the other things we had worked so hard for, the stuff it took so long to obtain, the material stuff we thought was important. The financial crisis was in full swing. At first, we lost the business, and then we started to lose our home. Without much of an income, we just didn't have enough money to make mortgage payments. We eventually were forced to leave. This was especially hard on my wife because this was the home where our kids woke up on Christmas mornings. It was the home where we had watched our family grow. We had more than a decade of memories there.

That loss was hard on all of us, especially me. I was the mortgage banker, the person who gives advice to others about their mortgage and financial affairs. Now I had just lost my home to foreclosure. One of the worst parts, at first, was the public humiliation. In our area, foreclosures go on Public Notice. That means they are broadcast in the local newspaper and posted on the paper's website with your name and home address for the entire county to see.

It was another blow to my pride and ego. This wasn't supposed to be happening to me. The grief and despair hit another level I didn't think was possible. I couldn't have even imagined this would ever happen to us. Things were really starting to compound in our lives now.

As the family provider, the loss of the business was very hard on me. I worked so hard for so many years to save the money for that venture. That wasn't even the hardest hit. My Green Book, and all I had thought about, worked for and focused on for many years, now seemed like one huge failure. It seemed like it was literally all for nothing. To say that I was feeling worthless, defeated, and depressed would be a massive understatement.

At the same time, there was a giant lurking in the shadows of my marriage that would soon rear its ugly head, ultimately putting my marriage to the test.

chapter four

Riding My Bike

Freedom On Two Wheels

When I was a kid, I loved to ride my bike. It gave me the freedom I did not have in any other way. My parents controlled when I woke up, what I ate, when I could hang out with my friends, etc. Obviously those are good things. Kids need structure. But the one thing I had complete freedom over was what happened when I was on my bike. My best memories are from Old Farms subdivision where my friends, brothers, and I would ride in packs. Sometimes just riding to ride, other times we would build ramps and see who could jump the farthest. It was our ticket to freedom, albeit very limited freedom. We still had rules on where we could ride to and when we had to be home, but in our lives that space and time was enormous.

I sometimes believe our adult lives have too much structure. We have a certain time to be at work and, generally, we are told what to do and when to do it. The responsibilities and the commitments we choose to take on can be all consuming at times. It's almost as if we get so busy living that we push the joy and excitement right out of our lives.

The affinity for riding my bike re-emerged in early high school. At that time, I didn't really know many other people who rode, so most of the time I would ride by myself. However, there was one influence in my life that made a big impact on my curiosity for cycling. My girlfriend's dad, Jim, had done quite a bit of riding and would sometimes talk about it. He was also a subscriber to *Outside* magazine. Every time I went over to their house, I made sure I read as many of the articles as I could. I was definitely born with a strong sense of adventure; I loved seeing the stories of what people were doing outdoors. Kayaking, cycling, hiking—all of it called to me. Its pull felt so natural. I loved being outdoors and experiencing new things. I didn't realize it at the time, but most of all I loved to challenge myself, to see what could be done.

I didn't ride for many years, but I got back into it in my late 30s. I always wanted to mountain bike, but I was out of shape and overweight. I could hardly pedal more than a couple of miles without stopping. I did some running before I got back into cycling, and it took me almost two years to run a 5k without stopping. You could say that I was consistently inconsistent. Shortly after that, I reconnected with some old friends who rode. I started going with them occasionally. I realized how much fun it really was. When something is fun, it's much easier to do because it doesn't seem like work. I stuck with it and really started to look forward to my rides.

A Warm, Sunny Morning

It was a warm, sunny morning in Michigan. With the Great Lakes, it's always a little humid and muggy in the summertime. This day was a little different, however. It was warm but comfortable, not muggy at all. Even though I was comfortable on the outside, I was uneasy on the inside. I got my bike out of the garage to ride before work, just like many mornings.

I hadn't always started my days this way. Oh, in years past I wanted to work out or get some type of exercise in the mornings, but I just never seemed to get around to it. I knew if I was ever going to get in shape, it had to be done then. Evenings just didn't work. It was family time, the kids had homework, they also had sports practice, and we had dinner to make. The list of busyness was endless at that time of day.

About a year earlier, I decided to make a real effort to get back into shape. For the first time in my adult life, I had actually stuck with it. I lost some weight and was feeling pretty good about my physical accomplishments, but something on the inside wasn't sitting quite right with me. I could feel it that morning. A sense of uneasiness had been growing for the past several weeks. I knew what it was, but I didn't want to confront it.

For quite some time, I could feel God gently tugging at me to spend more time with Him. I liked my schedule; I finally got some consistency in it. I just wasn't sure where I was willing to fit Him in. Honestly, I was more concerned with what I was going to find if I did go deeper with Him. I was a little afraid.

> I made a decision that
> morning that would radically
> change my life forever.

I did something different that morning. The gentle tug had now grown into a pull that I could no longer ignore. Unlike the past, I didn't shut it down this time. I yielded to it. I made a decision that morning that would radically change my life forever. It was a simple one. I decided that every time I rode my bike without friends along, it was God time. That meant every single ride I would spend time with Him. I didn't really know where to start, so I prayed about it. The Lord showed me what to do. He led me to some amazing audiobooks, faith songs, audio sermons, and more.

Mountain Biking With Jesus

My relationship with God grew very quickly. We were spending a lot of time together. At that point, I was riding three to four days a week, almost an hour each day. One day I drove an hour away from home to ride some back roads and mountain bike trails for different scenery. When I got there, I realized I left my earbuds at home. I wasn't going back for them, so I jumped on my bike and said a little prayer. I said, "Lord, show me what to do today. I don't have any music or my audiobook, and I was planning on a long ride." A thought came over me, "What if I just talk to Him for the entire ride?" I thought, "Okay, I guess I'm going freestyle today." It ended up being an amazing day and the start of some of my favorite types of rides. From that point, I called them "freestyle rides."

I rode and carried on an open-ended conversation with God. I did all the talking, but I could really sense His presence that day. I was in a state of gratitude as I rode the dirt roads of Oakland County, Michigan. I saw the houses, rolling hills, and wildlife from a completely different perspective. It may sound weird, but I think He was showing me a small piece of how He views the world. I saw the beauty of the rolling hills and the craftsmanship of His artistic hand in the lakes and streams.

As I looked at each home, I couldn't help but think about the people who lived there and how those homes provided safety, security, and warmth for His children. I saw the wildlife differently, too. The flocks of geese flying overhead are simply engineering masterpieces that He created, all flying in perfect order and at the same pace, taking turns leading.

Going freestyle became one of my favorite types of rides. The greatest part about riding my bike was no interruptions. I put my phone on silent mode and focused 100 percent on our time together. My relationship with Him started to explode; it was growing so fast and I wanted more.

The best part is, it was never forced. I never felt like I had to ride and do the God thing. As we began to spend more time together, I started to look forward to our rides. I didn't have any preconceived notions, nor did I know anything about actually communicating with God. I hadn't really given it much thought before. But, as this went on, I was amazed at how close we can actually get to Him.

For years, my day started the same way: I would wake up and immediately check emails, social media, or watch the news. What a difference it made when I made the decision to choose to start my day with something positive, like prayer and reading the Bible instead of filling my mind with the negative stuff in the news. I made that decision shortly after I started riding consistently with God. During my morning prayer time, I would ask Him, "What do you want me to listen to or talk about today, Lord?" I would then go through audiobooks or my music playlists and I would stop on the one that jumped out at me. Then I prayed about it for a few seconds. Once I felt His peace, I knew that's what he wanted me to listen to on that day's bike ride. I still do that today. As this process went on month after month, I realized something: He was teaching me a second language, one that many others had spoken before. I just never knew this language existed.

Learning a Second Language

In years past, when I occasionally went to church, I heard about the importance of a relationship with God. I never really knew what that meant or how to go about it. I had also heard people say they could hear His voice and sense His will for their lives. I didn't really think that applied to me. I just figured that was for the "holy" people. I definitely did not consider myself one, and I still don't.

Before I truly started to develop a relationship with God, I was good at shutting Him down. Especially when I wasn't doing the right things in life, I knew it. Sometimes I could feel Him questioning me about my choices, and I didn't like it. Other times, I could feel His presence and I loved it. I could gradually sense Him communicating with me.

At first, I didn't necessarily know His gentle whispers and nudges. When you spend just enough time with Him, however, you clearly start to recognize it. Those gentle whispers and nudges are easy to miss or disregard as passing thoughts or notions. The normal response at first is, "Was that my voice or His going off in my head?" Sometimes that thought or voice can be confusing. Feelings are driven by emotion, and emotions often lead us astray. It's a feeling, but it's more of a knowing. Generally, if you have to ask if it was your voice or His, it probably wasn't His. That is not to be confused with the resistance to what you hear, though. Sometimes we clearly hear but don't want to acknowledge what was said. I once heard a pastor talking about communing with God, describing it this way: "You're sensing it more than hearing it." (See John 14:16-17.)

I believe the key is to let go and let Him lead. There is often a sense of peace that comes with communicating with Him. The easiest way to think about it is to follow the peace. I've often thought that communicating with God is like learning a second language. It's all very foreign at first and you start by learning just a few words. Those words turn into sentences, and then you eventually learn to speak the language. The process doesn't happen right away. It takes time.

Communicating with God isn't nearly as mystical as it may seem. When my kids were younger, they went to a local preschool. Every time I picked them up, it was easy to detect where my son or daughter were in the room, even among all the other kids talking, playing, or even screaming. I knew their voices, mannerisms, and cries. It's simple: The same holds true with God. The more time you spend with the Lord, the more you can distinguish His voice. It's almost as if He placed a computer chip in every single human being, all six billion or so of us.

That chip is activated the moment we accept His son, Jesus, into our hearts as our liberator in life and place our trust and faith in Him.

However, the chip can have interference if we allow it. This is where sin comes in. Sin is the interference that gets in our communication lines with God. Simply put, the less sin in our lives, the less interference we will have in our relationship with Him. None of us are sinless. That's where grace and forgiveness come in. God always meets us where we're at. In other words, He doesn't expect perfection. He just wants us to keep pursuing Him. Distractions also play a big role in our ability to communicate with Him. The minds He gave us are amazing machines, capable of carrying out almost any task we focus on. Our job is to harness and direct that focus into worthwhile areas by using His guidance.

I've often thought, "Lord, why don't you just talk to us audibly so that we can hear you loud and clear? It would be easier for us to communicate and easier for You to tell us what You want us to do or the answer to our questions." God occasionally chooses to communicate with us that way but, by far, the majority of the time He does not. When He chooses to speak to us, He often does it in whispers and nudges. His ways are not our ways. We can sit back and wait a lifetime for Him to speak our language or we can open our minds and hearts and begin to learn His language.

When He chooses to speak to us, He often does it in whispers and nudges.

I believe He gives us just enough so we still lean into Him and pursue Him. He wants that relationship with us. This is how He chooses to interact with us, and there is reason for it. I certainly don't know that reason, but maybe someday when I meet Him, I'll know. Honestly, it doesn't really matter.

Listening to Prayers

I like to do what I call "listening prayers." This is pretty simple. During your Bible reading and prayer time, listen more than talk. That's it.

I always start by asking God to help me clear out the material world and bring in His world. Then I pause and take a couple of deep breaths. In my mind, my worries and problems leave me. I don't always focus on each one. I have found that if I do, worry sets in deeper. Sometimes I'll even try to visualize it, like a scene from a movie where a passenger-less airplane's side door opens while flying at 25,000 feet. The cabin contents get sucked out of the plane immediately. Visualize all your problems being instantly sucked out. Once your mind is clear, then begin to focus on Him, nothing else. This took me some time to become more efficient at. Once you get it down, the whole process only takes about 15 to 20 seconds.

Next, talk to Him. He already knows every thought on your mind anyway, so there's no need to firehose Him with everything. There are only two questions you need to ask, then shut up and wait.

1. What is it that you want me to know?

2. What is it that you want me to do?

Now, just listen. Don't allow your mind to bounce around in other areas. Just relax, listen, and follow the peace. All this may sound like some new-age stuff, but it's not at all. It's old age. The Christians had it first. Jesus spent many hours alone with His father in quiet prayer time. Don't forget the key ingredient: faith. If you don't believe that He will communicate with you this way, then you may never experience His presence to the fullest.

Let me also say that God is not a genie in a bottle who can be summoned on command. Some days when I do this, He comes through loud and clear. Other days, I hear nothing at all. He is often silent for a reason. This silence can last anywhere from minutes to days, sometimes longer. He is our Lord, Creator of all things. His ways are not our ways. Be open to where He leads you. He may put a person or a thought on your mind. He may put a Bible verse or a solution to a problem you have on your mind. Don't overthink it. Just simply relax and be open to His lead. The more you do so, the more you will learn to detect His voice. Don't look for loud shouts. Remember, the Lord most often speaks in whispers and nudges.

Safeguards

It is exciting to take this newfound communication with God to the next level. However, it's important to be sure that you're hearing from God and not yourself, or worse, someone or something else. Here are a few things to ask yourself. Make sure the message is from Him.

1. Does what I'm hearing line up with Scripture?

2. Is it helping me get closer to God and or make positive changes in my life?

3. Does it bring glory to God?

This is important to know. He will convict your heart if there's an area of your life that may need change. However, He never uses guilt, fear, or what I call "toxic shame." You may feel healthy shame. That is different. It helps you correct wrongs, repent, and grow. Toxic shame is the little voice that tells you self-defeating lies. Those lies keep you stuck in destructive cycles that repeat themselves.

He only communicates in truth. Truth is the essence of what is real. It doesn't deal in falsehoods, masks, misrepresentations, or ulterior motives. God sees you as the true you. He sees you for who He created you to be, not who or what you may be right now.

He only communicates in truth.
Truth is the essence of what is real.

Spiritual Warfare

The more I kept riding my bike, the more an internal struggle began
to slowly grow inside me. I loved riding, but did I like it too much?
Was I starting to put that in front of God? The thought of doing that
really scared me. I didn't want any part of putting something in front
of God. I had already done a good enough job at that the past couple
of decades. I really looked forward to my time on the bike and with
God while riding, but there was this little voice in my head that kept
telling me otherwise. This little voice began to get louder. I could feel
its strength growing. It was telling me that I shouldn't be riding as much
and that if I really wanted to serve God, I should be taking that time
and doing something else. Furthermore, it was saying that you can stay
close to God by reading your Bible and praying at home. You don't need
to spend that much time with Him riding. It was also trying to redirect
my path by telling me, "If you really want to do the will of God, you
should be a pastor or missionary, anything but a guy who rides a bike."
I wasn't literally hearing voices in my head. It was more of a sense of an
internal guilt, and I didn't know where it was coming from.

I could clearly see how God was working through me at my job. I could
also clearly see the gifts others have and how they used them to serve
God and others. Those gifts included the ability to mechanically fix
things, preach a sermon, or create beautiful music or art. I just couldn't
help but think, "Why am I riding my bike?" Yes, it's for exercise, but I
was riding for more than just basic exercise. I seemed to have this deep
passion for it, though, that I can't explain. It just felt like that's what I
was supposed to do with every fiber of my being. But I kept thinking

to myself, "Lord, why are you having me ride? I just don't understand." That is part of the reason I yielded to the little voice inside of me that was telling me to stop riding. I couldn't see how it had anything at all to do with me helping God build His kingdom.

There seems to be this unwritten, unspoken thing that some people feel when they start to really grow spiritually in the Christian world. It's an underlying feeling of guilt that if you're serious about Christianity, you need to do God's work in a church or as a pastor or missionary. Anything less than that makes you some kind of second-class Christian. Nothing could actually be further from the truth, but I didn't know it then. I had prayed about it many times, but I had allowed that little voice to grow so strong I could no longer detect God's voice among all my thoughts and feelings. One day I was on board with riding and the next day I was going to sell my bike. It was a mess. This battle inside of me had been going on for many weeks. It was really starting to frustrate me, and I couldn't seem to solve it in ways I had in the past—strictly through prayer and reading my Bible. This was a time in my life that I hadn't learned to be in sync with God yet. I knew I needed outside help.

Sometimes we need others to help us, encourage us, and keep us on the right path. One of the ways God speaks to us is through people. Every week, I meet with several guys from my church for an accountability and prayer group. I took my dilemma to them. They had the experience to help and told me about spiritual warfare. I had heard of this before but had never experienced it in any up-close-and-personal way. Spiritual warfare can take on many faces. In my case, Satan was directly attacking me to stop doing what I was doing. He was so sneaky and deceitful about it. He had actually made me feel guilty for doing what I truly felt I was supposed to do. The amazing gift was that God had allowed him to let me struggle. I wouldn't have experienced the power of the devil's capabilities and see what his attacks looked like if God hadn't allowed me to struggle. We are often in such battles and don't even know it.

Many times, God will allow us to struggle, not to hurt us but to help us. Be patient. Let Him do His good work in you.

chapter five

It Got Worse Before It Got Better

Another Turning Point

My relationship with God was growing. My relationship with my wife was not. I was still riding several days a week and spending more time with God, but I still had a lot of growing to do. Maturing with God is so different from maturing without Him. It is a process that takes time and has to be done slowly, one layer at a time. It has to be guided by Him, not us. Each of us has different mindsets, viewpoints, and experiences in life that consciously or subconsciously drive our decisions. God was slowly rewiring mine. Finally, for the first time in my life, I was letting him rewire me.

Problems in our past were resurfacing. The nonstop pressure that we had been going through the past few years was starting to compound.

Everyone seems to handle pressure in different ways. Some of us internalize it by blaming ourselves—I was in that category. When things get tough, we immediately go into problem-solving mode to fix the issue. The problem with that is, we often end up carrying the burden alone—partially because we may not want to yield our pride to ask for help and partially because we may not want to give up control. That could seemingly affect the outcome we are working toward.

We want to just fix things, but sometimes we can't fix things on our own. This trait was driving me to focus less on my marriage and more on trying to get financially stable again. Our ongoing, dire financial position was bringing a lot of pressure into our home. My flawed logic was that if I could fix that, then the other problems would get much better. Others seem to handle pressure by externalizing it, and that was my wife. She was looking to other things and other people to help her cope with the mess. As the separation grew, so did the problems. This was a recipe for disaster.

I felt like I was in a war. Our marriage had succumbed to a multitude of mortar shells and enemy fire that was so fierce it just simply couldn't survive. All of this chaos led us to look elsewhere instead of where we should have been focused. In short, we looked to other things instead of God. All of this friction finally came to a head. Unfortunately, it led to a betrayal that, in my mind, was completely unforgivable. She left our home, and I believed I had no choice but to file for divorce.

A few days later, I called a past client who was also a divorce attorney. We shared a couple of minutes of the usual small talk, and then I told him why I was calling. He knew a little bit about me, that I had been going through some financial troubles, but I don't think he knew much else about me or my wife. What he said next shocked me

Before I had the chance to share even one sentence about what had happened, he said, "Let me stop you right there, Aaron. Let me guess. You're in your early 40s, your kids are getting older and are out of the house or will be soon. They're probably late teens to early 20s. You and your wife have been growing apart. That is the most dangerous time in many marriages. Couples who let their lives revolve around their kids and not around a good relationship with each other first are most vulnerable. When the kids get older and don't need mom and dad as much anymore, the commonality the parents share is gone. I see it all the time. It's sad to say, but that is almost half of my business as a divorce attorney. One or both parents look to other things and sometimes other people to fill that void. Then resentment sets in; finger-pointing and blame starts. Then, unless stopped, it slowly goes downhill from there. Am I close?"

I just sat there in a mild state of shock. There was about 10 to 15 seconds of silence before I could even utter a word. I didn't know what to say. My first thought was about how I wasn't calling for a psychological analysis of my life. What made him think he could even say something like that to me? The fact was, he was right on target, but that thought quickly left my mind.

I couldn't get over how blatantly obvious this dysfunction had been to someone who didn't know me or my wife at all. How could this have happened to us when we didn't even recognize it for what it truly was? We did recognize our many problems, but we didn't know the right steps to correct the situation. My eyes opened in that conversation, and I have shared that story many times with others, hoping it will help other married couples in a similar situation.

As reality set in in the coming days, my pity party reached new heights. I could only think, "First my life's dream, my business, had been taken away from me, then my home, the house we raised our children in, was gone." After that, almost all of my material possessions were stripped away. Even though my wife and I weren't getting along, I was grateful because I still had my marriage. Now that was gone, too. What else could possibly happen?

All I could think was, "I have nothing left, God. Nothing!" This was the fifth year in a row of some type of catastrophe in my life. The financial and personal roller coaster seemed unending. Every time I started to feel like things might get better or I was making progress, another crash in my life came along. I felt like I was literally starting to live out the story of Job.

By the grace of God, this pity party didn't last long. God's sense of peace and comfort carried me through. Little did I know at the time, but He was molding and shaping me into the person He created me to be.

It's Not Fair

Life is so seemingly unfair. Why do bad things happen to good people? It's confusing when those things happen. The truth is, in those times, you are at a crux, a fork in the road. The decisions you make next will amplify the final results in one direction or another. We can get mad at God or whomever we believe is responsible or we can use this event to draw upon God's strength, wisdom, and peace. In short, we can choose to lean into Him or lean away from Him.

The absolute worst things in my life—loss of family members, loss of health, financial ruin, divorce and so on—have all resulted in amazing peace and clarity when I decided to lean into God. The times I chose to lean away from Him didn't end well. They were cold, bitter, and lonely. Because we are so consumed by the circumstances of the moment, it is often difficult for us to see what God is really doing.

Because we are so consumed
by the circumstances of the moment,
it is often difficult for us to see
what God is really doing.

Church Three Weeks Later

The first couple of weeks after filing for divorce were the hardest. My soon-to-be ex-wife and I had been together for almost 20 years. It was a mixture of emotions. One minute I was sad, one minute I was happy, the next minute I didn't know what I was feeling. Honestly, it wasn't just the downfall of the marriage that was tough. We had three children together and they were each at different points in their lives. They each needed us in a different way at that time. That dynamic made the situation even harder.

It was weird. As depressed as I was, I was also relieved. A massive weight was slowly being lifted off me. The strange part was I didn't even realize the magnitude of that weight until I stepped away from the situation. This had been a long time coming, and I knew it, but I just didn't want to admit it. As strange as it sounds, I was beginning to see God work heavily in my life. I could slowly feel layers of doubt and fear leave me. It's amazing how He can do His best work when we are at our lowest point. I think this is in part because we don't allow Him in when times are good.

I started attending church more frequently. I woke up one Sunday about three weeks after filing for divorce. This day was a little different. I thought about not going, but I could just feel that He wanted me there. I prayed about it as I drove into the parking lot of Lakeport Wesleyan Church. I asked God to open my heart and mind for that morning's message.

When the service started, I could really feel His presence. It was so strong in me that I couldn't ignore it. The worship team started their usual routine of singing and getting the service kicked off. What happened next was the start of something that would change me instantly and permanently before I left church.

The worship leader, Maralee, started singing, but then she paused. Instead of singing, she began to speak. As the band played in the background, Maralee said, "You know you're in God's will when things seem to be flowing naturally around you. Everything seems to be happening with ease and nothing is forced." She said exactly what was under the surface of my thoughts. I had no idea that I was living that out in real time the past three weeks until she said those words. I hadn't thought about it that way. Every single issue I had been going through seemed to be miraculously handled by God. This is not to say there weren't problems or bad days. There were plenty of long, lonely, depressing days.

He was guiding me through each in spirit and in love. He was navigating me through this time in my life. I was again overcome with emotion and gratitude. As I fought back tears, all I could think was, "Who am I that the God of the universe, Creator of all things known, would want to be so personal with me?" What happened next can only be described as an amazing miracle. His presence here on earth, the Holy Spirit, was about to make an up-close-and-personal visit.

After the music, the pastor got right into his talk for the day. He talked about forgiveness and how those who don't forgive carry a heavy burden. This burden often turns into bitterness, and the bitterness leads to a hard heart, which is more closed off from love, acceptance, and kindness. A hard heart has trouble letting the light of Jesus in. As he went on, I could literally feel the Holy Spirit whirling about me, penetrating my spirit and soul. It was almost as if He was cleaning me from the inside out. In a fraction of a second, He showed me a vision in great detail. It literally happened that fast, but I could recall in micro detail what He showed me.

He showed me what happened in my life and in my marriage. He gave me instant clarity, understanding, and overwhelming peace about the situation. He cleared the slate and gave me a completely new start, all in an instant. He completely removed the depression I had been feeling. It was gone at that moment and has never returned, even to this day. Again, it was all I could do to fight back tears and not lose my composure. As I walked out of church that day, I could strongly feel what He wanted me to do. I stopped in my tracks and forgave two people before I got to my car. I forgave myself for not being the husband I could have been. I texted my wife and forgave her.

The hand of God touched my life that day as the weight of the world was lifted off my back. The man who got out of the car before church wasn't the same man who got back in it. After church that morning, I never had bad days again. I had some bad moments here and there, but never again did I have a deep, depressing day.

> The man who got out of the car before church wasn't the same man who got back in it.

Starting From Scratch

While growing up, my stepdad ran a charter boat service for a few years. We would spend many weekends fishing for salmon on the Great Lakes. This was way before modern technology could detect approaching storms. We often just had to keep an eye on the sky. Sometimes while out in the middle of the lake, these storms would come up fast, seemingly out of nowhere. They would hit hard, and you better be ready. First, the wind would pick up, and then the gently rolling waves would gradually grow to what we called white caps. That meant things were starting to get serious. Sometimes the storms would hit so fast and hard that we almost didn't have time to react. The boat would be a helpless victim randomly thrown around by the waves. If

57

you stayed out too long and got caught in a storm like that, you might not make it back. My life seemed like one big storm for the past five years. Every time I turned around, another set of waves battered my life. Only, I couldn't make it back to shore.

I really began to question who I was on a much deeper level. I had allowed God to peel back one layer at a time and deal with each issue in my life on its own. Once one was done, then He'd move on to the next and the next. I wasn't sure I had any layers left for Him to work on. Sure, it was uncomfortable but, strangely enough, over time you grow used to changing and growing like that. I felt as if I was starting my life from scratch. This was a scary but good place to be.

Things were starting to slowly get better. I was working at the original mortgage company I had started with many years earlier. Things were going well there and I was grateful. However, I couldn't help but give in to negative thoughts, such as "Here I am in midlife and everything I thought I was ever going to be, have, or do is gone. Not a trace left." I had to rebuild from ground zero and with nothing to show for the last couple of decades. The truth was, I did have something to show for it, something that God had crafted, shaped, molded, and honed during those five years.

Your Superpower

I loved watching cartoons on Saturday mornings when I was a kid. Yes, that was the only time they were on TV—just Saturday mornings. One of my favorite shows was "Super Friends." It had all my favorite superheroes: Batman, Robin, Aquaman, Wonder Woman, Superman, and more. Every episode was pretty much the same, but as a kid, I didn't care. There would be a bad guy who came to destroy the city. They would fight the bad guy. They'd get to the point where it looked like they were finally going to lose, then at the end, one of the superheroes would come in and save the day. Each hero had his or her own unique ability or power that no one else had. Often they had to rely on a hero who didn't have the same power as they did to get the job done. They needed to work together. Those were some great lessons for me as a kid. One of the messages was to try not to do it all by yourself. Sometimes we need to rely on others and sometimes we need to be the one whom others rely on. Those are also some great lessons for us adults.

I truly believe that each and every one of us has our own superpower. Every single person walking this earth has a unique ability, talent, passion, or skill that no one else has. God has created each and every one of us in His image. His image! No other creature that we know of in the universe can say that. He also created us individually. The Bible says He even has every single hair on our heads numbered (Luke 12:7 and Matthew 10:30). Each of us has been given our own unique gifts (1 Peter 4:10-11, Romans 12:6-8, 1 Corinthians 12:4-6). These are just a few of the verses that reference it. He has set the exact time and place in which we would each live (Acts 17:26). You do matter and your life is not a random coincidence.

The things God allowed to happen to me in the past five years were not so I would be torn down and stay down. They were permitted so I would be torn down and brought back up, rebuilt and better than ever. We often only think of Jesus as a God of love and compassion. While this is very true, He is also a God of power and one who knows how to use that power to create change, positive change. The more time I spent with Him while riding my bike, the more He was starting to show me what my superpower was. More importantly, He was showing me how to use it.

One of the things that has always come easy to me has been talking with or connecting with people. I am a pretty social person. Throw me in a room with a bunch of strangers and it's not a problem for me to come out with a new friend or two. The part of my personality that makes that easy for me is that I like to help people. I'm curious about their lives and what makes them tick. You could say I'm interested in them. This is one of my superpowers. Yes, I know it sounds strange, but it's true. Each of us has little things that come easy to us, we're passionate about, or can do really well. The problem with this trait is figuring out what to do with it besides make new friends.

As I grew closer to God, He showed me how I could use it to help others. The training grounds in which He showed me this was in my job. As I matured in my relationship with God, I started to view each and every customer who came to me to get a mortgage as individual children of God. Each one had a different story, background, and life circumstances. Many had some rough times in their lives—divorce, health or relationship problems. The list is endless. I could truly relate to them on a much different level after having gone through much of the same myself. He showed me how to take care of them, listen to them, be there for them, and help walk them through the often stressful process of buying a home. It's one small piece of someone's life, but it's an important one. Over time I grew to really try and put the love of Christ into each and every real estate transaction I was involved in. I have prayed for so many clients over the past several years. Most of the time they didn't even know that I was praying for them. I would see a need in their life somewhere and God would put it on my heart to help them in some way, even if it was something as simple as a friendly phone call or text from me giving them a word of encouragement. That simple shift in how I thought about my clients began to spill over into other areas of my life and other relationships as well. I gradually started working with and supporting a few local nonprofit organizations in my area. Those contributions began to grow as I learned to spend my time and resources giving back to my community.

A lady at my church loves to bake. She uses her superpower to make others feel important. She works at a local car dealership. Every time an employee has a birthday, she bakes them a cake. Imagine how special that makes them feel. She takes time out of her life for each and every individual employee. She doesn't even own the company. She's the receptionist there. Some of those employees may not have families that celebrate with them. Some may have no one in their lives acknowledge them.

What if your superpower was singing, building things, or helping the sick? What if you didn't do those things? Who would sing beautiful music for us all to hear, build our homes, or take care of us when we're sick? Don't waste the superpower God has given you. Use it to better the community you live in. When you do, watch and see what happens. Soon you will be the one who was given back the best gift: the gift of helping others.

chapter six

Pursuing a Dream ... His Way

A New Life Begins

My life carried on, this time as a single dad. I was adjusting to a new life, and all three of my children were learning to adjust, too. One son graduated and was living on his own in another part of the state; the other was just finishing his first year of college and still living at home. My daughter, the youngest, was a sophomore in high school. The kids moved in with me, and our new life began.

In the coming months, life got much better. My plan was pretty straightforward. I just wanted a simple life. We were renting a small house. I was looking to get some stability, and my main goal was to start looking for a home to buy. I had no desire to date anyone. I wasn't one of those bitter divorcees who wanted nothing to do with getting close to anyone again. I just didn't want the hassle. My life was simple and I wanted to keep it that way. Once again, God had other plans.

I have always felt the need to get better, to improve, no matter what I'm doing in life. This often comes in the form of reading. I especially enjoy reading books that help me live a better life or be a better person. One day I was reading a business book and I came across a section in a chapter where the author spoke about what he did when he decided that he wanted to get married. The funny thing was, he wasn't even dating anyone at the time, but he knew exactly what he wanted in his future spouse. Being the organized overachiever that he is, he wrote down an exact list of the qualities that person would have. He wrote all the details down, even what color hair he liked best. I got a chuckle out of it as I read. My only thought was, "I wish I had this book long ago." Ha! Then I thought about it for a minute, "That's actually a pretty good idea." The author was using this as an example of focus. You have to know exactly what you want before going after it. It's a great lesson. So just for fun, I grabbed a notepad and wrote down what my list would look like. I came up with six things in about five minutes.

Not too long after that, my friend Dave called and asked if I wanted to meet up with some of his friends. I had nothing else going on, so I said sure. There was someone named Michelle there, whom I seemed to have a lot in common with. Apparently I had met her before, but it was in a quick, passing conversation a few months earlier. The only reason I remembered her was because she was the flip-flop lady.

I was at a local concert the summer before when Dave introduced me to her and a few other friends. I only remembered her because she had a broken flip-flop, and she had a great attitude about it. It's not so easy to walk in a broken flip-flop. Michelle and I started to hang out as friends. She was widowed about a year and a half earlier and not really looking for any relationship. I was definitely not looking for one, either, but we both enjoyed each other's company and had fun when we went out.

We made it very clear to each other that we'd just be friends. After a while, we realized that we had a lot more in common than we originally thought. At first, I almost stopped the relationship because I could sense we were starting to like each other as more than friends. The strange thing was when I brought it to God in prayer, He gave me the warm feeling of peace I had come to know so well from Him. That feeling always meant His blessing. Even though I knew that, I couldn't bring myself to take this relationship seriously at first. It was just too soon.

I passed those feelings off as me just not thinking straight and how it was a rebound from the divorce. As time went on, we simply couldn't deny the connection. Every single time I prayed about it, it was as if God would push me closer to her. I even prayed for Him to end this relationship so that I could just forget about her and move on with my life. I really liked Michelle and could see myself with her in the future, but I was afraid—afraid that tragedy would somehow strike again.

Via De Cristo
Around Christmastime that year, my pastor had been telling me about a faith weekend called Via De Cristo. It was a three-day retreat at a church, spending time in prayer and Bible sessions around the clock. No phones or contact with the outside world were allowed. The entire weekend was designed to bring you up close and personal with God. When my pastor asked me if I wanted to go, I think I said yes before he even finished his sentence. A month later, we got in his car and headed up to Saginaw, Michigan, for the trip.

It was an amazing weekend. The timing in my life was perfect. I thought my relationship with God was close before I went. I even got closer to Him there than I ever thought possible. I came home with a renewed and strengthened sense of faith, one that stays with me even to this day. While there, I couldn't help but think of two things a lot: a cycling adventure I really wanted to do and Michelle. I asked God to remove those items from my life if He didn't want me to go in that direction. That weekend was the first time in my life I truly started to put His will in front of my own. Notice that I said "started," because putting His will in front of ours is a process, a long one. I still struggle with it, even as I write this book.

When I got home the first morning after Via De Cristo, I woke up, got some coffee, and sat down at my kitchen table to spend some time with my best friend, God. As I sat there that morning, I could feel His strong, very strong presence. He immediately asked me to write something down. I grabbed my notepad from the weekend and He told me, "No! Don't write it down on that." His response took me by surprise. He gently said to my mind, "Write it on a separate piece of paper." I thought, "Why are you asking me to do this?" But I knew He had His reasons.

The verse He had me write down that day was Jeremiah 29:11 (NIV): *"For I know the plans I have for you, declares the Lord, plans to prosper you and not to harm you, plans to give you hope and a future."* "Whoooaa!" I thought. I was amazed at the sense of hope I could feel. What was that writing thing on a separate piece of paper all about? Wooow!!! I had no idea what it meant or where He was going to take me, but I knew one thing: it had to do with Michelle. Something told me to get my list out, the one I had written after reading the book about the guy who wanted to get married. I looked at it before with her in mind, but this time I had a new set of eyes on it.

The clarity I had about myself, my relationship with God, and whom He wanted me to be with was obvious. As I went down the list, Michelle met every single thing and more. At this point, she and I had grown pretty close. The signal to be with her was so loud and clear in every way that I couldn't possibly ignore it. Within a few days, I asked her to marry me. We were married soon afterward.

It's amazing how well God knows us. He knows us so much better than we could ever even know ourselves. For months I couldn't find the piece of paper that I wrote Jeremiah 29:11 on. God knew that I would dwell on it too much. That's why He didn't allow me to write it in my regular notebook. He wanted it separate so I would stay on the path He wanted me on. I had a good track record of getting in front of God, not being patient, and waiting for His timing instead of mine.

He knew what I needed in Michelle, too. Even though I wanted no part of any relationship, He had other plans. I was building a new life now, the right way this time: one with God first instead of me first. I was learning to put Him first in every area of my life, my family, my work and even my fitness. I was still consistently riding my bike with Him. That area of my life was taking a new turn. He put a dream in me that was about to come to fruition, one that I could have never thought of attempting. This time I would pursue a dream His way, not mine.

Pursuing Your Dream

My wife, Michelle, is afraid of spiders. She can't stand them and literally has to execute every single one she sees on the spot. Every time she smashes even a tiny one, she looks at me and says, "Honey, I just saved our lives again!" We all have things we are afraid of. I have had one thing that has plagued me for years—the fear of dying with a dream in my heart. I want to get to heaven, be able to look God in the face, and hear Him say, "Well done, faithful servant." I believe that every single one of us, without exception, was created for a purpose. I believe that God created each of us with individual gifts, passions, talents, and strengths to accomplish these things. The Bible has many Scriptures that reference this. Discovering and building on our talents gives us purpose. Having purpose gives us hope. Hopelessness may be one of the leading causes of drug abuse, alcoholism, and divorce. No hope leads to mediocrity. Mediocrity could be our No. 1 enemy. It's sneaky. It creeps up on us, and we don't even know it. It can sometimes be a comfortable place, but it's oddly uncomfortable at the same time. Unfortunately, for many of us, it's just comfortable enough to stay there.

I believe that every single one of us,
without exception,
was created for a unique purpose.

I've always been a dreamer. For as long as I can remember, I've been dreaming about what could be accomplished. As my relationship grew with Christ, so did the magnitude of my dream. He began to pull and stretch me to see the world in a different way. He showed me how just one person could have an enormous impact. I began to realize that my dreams and goals could help others, too. I never knew the right way to go about pursuing these things until I truly had a relationship with Christ. Over time, I came to realize a formula of sorts that would help me discover, refine, and pursue my aspirations or, should I say, His aspirations.

Sometimes it's hard to really know what God's dreams are for us. Chances are you probably already have something on your heart you want to be a part of or something you want to accomplish. That's a good starting point. Often God puts dreams in us well before we even know Him or know who He is. One way to go about discovering if your dream is the right thing to do or not is by asking yourself: Do I have a passion to do this? Do I have the gifts to carry it out?

An example of what would typically not work: You want to be a famous singer (passion), but you can't carry a tune to save your life (no gift). That's not to say you can't possibly learn, but chances are, this may not be the right direction for you. An example of what would work: You want to become an elementary school teacher. You have the desire to do it (passion) and you're an extremely caring and patient person (gift). There are always exceptions to every rule. This simple formula by no means gives you a definitive answer. It simply gets you started in the

right direction. Once you know the direction of your goal, you'll want
to be sure it is in sync with what God wants for your life.

Being In Sync

We are emotional beings, and our pursuits can often lead us astray.
You see it every single day. Many of us pursue things in life for various
reasons: the need to fit in, the need to gain wealth, or the need to
validate our worth to a parent or teacher. The list is endless. This is
where we need to pause, because this is a critical point in our journey.
This is where we want to be sure that we are in unity, or what I like to
call "in sync," with God. As my relationship with Him grew over time,
I realized that I had somewhat accidentally discovered a process to go
through when I wanted God's input in my life. This formula will help
you start to discover God's will or direction for your life.

The topic of trying to know God's will for our lives can stir a mixture of
emotions and opinions. On a basic level, His first will is for us to know
Him. That starts by accepting Jesus, His son, as our Lord and Savior.
This is the foundation on which all other areas of your life—especially
your ability to have a relationship with Him—rest. He has other intents
for your life. If you really want to know them, just look at the Ten
Commandments. With many other decisions, He gives us free rein to
do what we want.

Beyond that, He has other intents for
your life. If you really want to know them,
just look at the Ten Commandments.
With many other decisions, He gives us
free rein to do what we want.

Yes, we all want to know what God wants for us, but it's beyond that. Think of it this way. If you owned a business with someone, wouldn't you consult with them before making large company decisions? You absolutely would, because you are partners. God is more than someone whom we read about in a book, visualize on a symbol, or hear about at church on Sundays. He's a living entity who absolutely wants to be in harmony with His creation. I invite Him into my life because He is my Father. I regard Him as my absolute best friend and I love Him. He gives us the free will to invite Him in or not. I choose to let Him in because I want His influence and His input in my life.

The following eight-step guide is how I approach receiving God's input. I have gone through this cycle hundreds of times over the years, using it in many facets of my life and in dozens of situations. I have used it in my relationships with others. I have used it in solving problems. I have used it in good times and bad. I hope that you, too, will use it as your guide.

1. **THOUGHTS**—You have a thought or an idea. This can be anything in your life. It could be something small, like handling a conflict with a friend or co-worker. It could also be something large, like your dream of someday starting a nonprofit for a cause that you're passionate about.

2. **PRAYERS**—Pray about whether you should act on this thought or idea. Open your heart and mind to Him. Remember, He is your loving Father and already knows what you're thinking. Don't be afraid to ask Him things, for example, how he feels about it or how He wants you to view it. Pray about what related Scriptures to read. When you read those Scriptures, learn to go off of your convictions instead of your emotions. There is a very clear difference.

3. **SCRIPTURE**—Search Scripture to be sure your thought or idea lines up with God's word and His character. There are plenty of examples of these in His word, the Bible. The Bible is the number one way God speaks to us. Just read His word and see what He has to say. I like to view the Bible as a letter, of sorts, that God has left us. In this letter, He gives us all kinds of guidelines to live by, wisdom to call on, and inspiration to keep us going during hard times. Meditate on His word. If there's something you don't understand, don't be afraid to wrestle with it. Ask Him to reveal its meaning to you.

4. **MOTIVES**—Does the outcome only benefit you? Ask God in prayer to reveal to you your true motives in this matter. Ask Him to reveal the ones you can't see and may be hidden in the caverns of your heart. Sometimes we say or do things based on the wrong motives, and we don't even know it until it's too late.

5. **PEACE**—Follow the peace. When making a decision, do you have peace about the situation? The more I engaged with this cycle, the more I became sensitive to the Father. This concept was not detectable to me too much at first. I had trouble knowing if the feelings I got were from me or from God. As I went through this many times and in many areas of my life, I really began to sense God's peace. The peace that He provides is very real and detectable. It has become a prominent factor for me. In some scenarios, if I don't feel peace about a situation, I often don't move forward. We have to learn to develop patience and let His good work come to fruition. There is an old saying, "If the devil can't get in front of you to stop you, he'll get behind and push you quickly through it." Peace can't be our only guide, though.

6. **WISDOM AND DISCERNMENT**—You will often get no feeling of peace or anything at all about many situations, and

that's normal. This is where wisdom and discernment come in. Wisdom is a beautiful gift that God gives us. He provides this to help us do the right thing and make the right decisions. Ask God for wisdom and discernment in your prayer time. This is a very important part of learning to be in sync with the Father.

7. **FAITH**—Whatever path you choose, you have to act on it in faith. Many times you will not have all of the answers to make an educated decision. In some situations, even wisdom is not enough. Sometimes the only thing to do is to simply go on faith. This is the hardest part for many of us. It can be very scary, especially the first several times you engage with this cycle. For some of you, the longer you have been in an established religion or tradition in how you interact with God, the harder this concept may or may not be for you to grasp. You'll have to be willing to see and interact with God in a different way. I know many people who can quote the Bible from cover to cover, but they can't honestly say they have an actual relationship with the Father. The word "relationship" is defined as "the state of being connected." One of the main purposes of this book is to move God from your head to your heart. In other words, one must not only have knowledge of Him but also have a connection with Him. If you don't believe you can be in sync with Him this much, you are right—you won't be. If you believe that you can, you are right—you will be. It takes faith. Trust that He has your best interests in mind. This doesn't mean sitting back and waiting for something to magically happen. Oftentimes, action on our part is how He reveals the right path.

8. **OUTCOME**—Here's where many of us need to be deprogrammed. We are used to putting food in the microwave and taking it out exactly as we expect within a precise amount of time. That may work in making popcorn, but it is not at all

Pursuing a Dream ... His Way

how God works. If you are truly in sync with Him, you have to allow His will to reign supreme over your will in all matters. In other words, what you want is important, but what He wants has to come first. Our job is to simply be submissive. When we truly learn to be submissive to God, that's when our relationship with Him flourishes beyond our imagination. After you step out in faith with this process, you will eventually see results. Sometimes this means that you have to wait. Yes, I said *wait*. I know that's hard to do, but in many instances it is critical to wait for His direction. I have found that God gives us plenty of free rein to make our own decisions. He doesn't seem to have this set rigid plan that involves trying to figure out what He wants us to do every minute of every day. Personally, I have found that He warns me or tells me what *not* to do more often than what to do. After you step out in faith with this process, you will eventually see results (see Hebrews 5:14).

You won't use all eight of these elements for every matter in your life. I have found that the larger issues in life require drawing from more of this list. As this process is repeated, you will begin to see results. You can then go back and see where you may have stayed in or out of sync with God. In turn, this constant interaction with God will help you begin to connect with Him on a much deeper level—one that goes way beyond words, ideas, or thoughts. You can only learn this with many repetitions; there are no shortcuts.

Here's an example of how to apply these steps:

You're in a conversation with a friend or co-worker and they say something that doesn't sound right. You can think to yourself quickly, "What are my motives or my thoughts on this? Is what I'm thinking in line with God's word?" It's okay to say a quick prayer and ask God, "Lord, am I viewing this situation correctly? Please give me thoughts and words to say." This can all be done in a few

73

seconds. God doesn't require long, drawn-out prayers. Instead, three to four words will do. This can also apply to large decisions you have to make in life. You can run through the same sequence. Pray about it, ask what the Bible says about it, think about what your true motives are, apply wisdom, use discernment, and so on. As you do this, you're developing the capability to bring God into ALL areas of your life.

I love reading the book of John. One of the larger themes is the unity between Jesus and the Father. Jesus was the only one who ever mastered this cycle, and that is a vast understatement. I'm sure that Jesus' unity with the Father was on a much higher level than this. For the rest of us, it's a constant process we must work on every day. The more you do it, the easier and more effective it becomes. This may seem new and very foreign to you, but it's not. You engage with this cycle every day. In fact, you have your whole life, but you maybe just haven't been aware of it.

I was in this cycle when I made the decision to leave my job of ten years and become partners in the mortgage company. I went off track when I missed a couple of steps. One of them was the step about following the peace. I didn't have peace about the situation. The truth is, I could sense that, but I didn't even really know to look for that then. Simply put, I was not at all in sync with God at that time in my life.

Conversely, this process protected me when I was wrestling with stopping my bike rides. I'm certain that it would have eventually dramatically reduced my alone time with God. In hindsight, there are dozens of amazing things that God has brought into my and others' lives because of my decision to continue riding. I didn't understand what God was doing in my life at that time. I couldn't see how He was working, and it frustrated me. I simply had to wait on Him in faith, which was hard. With time, the right answer slowly came to me in several ways. One day during quiet time with God, in prayer and in the Bible, I made a final decision to continue riding. I had a massive sense of peace come over me about the situation while reading the book of Ecclesiastes. As I mentioned, *Another 20 Feet* may have never been written if I had made a quick decision—out of confusion or fear—and stopped riding. Just because you can't possibly see how God is working in your life doesn't mean He's not.

Just because you can't possibly see
how God is working in your life
doesn't mean He's not.

Over time, you will be absolutely amazed at how intimate and personal He will be with you. Remember to keep it simple. Don't try to overthink or overdo it by looking for some type of crazy, supernatural experience. Just stay in prayer and the Bible consistently. Be patient and work hard. Always remember this: Make your plans in pencil, but give God the eraser. (See 1 Thessalonians 5:17.)

Always remember this:
Make your plans in pencil,
but give God the eraser.

This is by no means an exhaustive explanation of how we can interact with the Father, and it is by no means the only way. It has worked very well for me, and it's easy to do. Now, go out and engage with your Creator.

Finding Marji

In the spring of 2016, a dream started to develop inside of me. I had been racing mountain bikes for about four years at a beginner-to-intermediate level. I mostly rode for fun and was definitely not a champion. On a good day, I would finish barely above mid-pack with the riders in my category.

I love a challenge and had been trying to get into the Leadville 100 mountain bike race in Colorado. There are so many riders trying to get in the race, they use a lottery system to determine who gets in. I've never even come close to doing anything like it before. It is a 100-mile off-road race in some of the highest elevations in Colorado. The oxygen deprivation alone can be debilitating, let alone also navigating 100 miles of mountain terrain. Many racers put all they have into the course, only to have their efforts end in the dreaded DNF (did not finish).

I was sitting at work one morning when my application results email came in. I just knew I was going to get in this year. The odds were in my favor, after all. How could I possibly not get it in three years in a row? If you're an athlete trying to get into events that operate on this kind of lottery system, you know the excitement of opening that email. It's the same anticipation a high school student has opening the acceptance/denial letter from their favorite college. It's the same anticipation we have when we've applied for a job and they call back after a great second interview. You get the picture.

I was afraid to open it. Was I in? Was I out? The first sentence was good. It said, "Dear Aaron." So far so good! The next sentence is where things began to unravel. It started with these five words, "We regret to inform you…" I had read enough, no need to go any further. I wasn't in again. It was so frustrating. I had been focusing on this race for three years now. It was what I thought about when I was unmotivated. Sometimes it was even what I thought about when I went to bed at night. I had prayed about it many times and really wanted it to happen. I love riding and I love the mountains in Colorado. My stepfather and I had done several archery elk hunts there in previous years. This time

I wanted to go back and conquer the mountains on my bike instead of on foot.

Another year, another denied application. The next couple of weeks were filled with frustration about not getting in, but it certainly wasn't the end of the world. Cycling is just one part of my life, probably fourth or fifth in importance. Nonetheless, it is a part of my life that is still significant. Riding keeps me healthy and focused on positive things. It gives me a goal and is a great outlet for stress. Most importantly, it helps me spend uninterrupted alone time with God. That has been by far the biggest blessing to come from it. It has been one of God's greatest workshops in my life. He has crafted, molded, and honed me there.

As I thought about what to do with my racing season, I could feel something begin to change inside of me. It wasn't anything I initiated. I just had a sense of peace on not getting into Leadville. I can't explain it; I was just okay with it from the inside out. Sometimes we say we're going to move on, but old thoughts or hang-ups still linger. It wasn't that way at all. I had prayed about it and simply gave it to God.

A couple of weeks later, I started looking at other races I could do in the upcoming season. Now that Leadville was out, the schedule was wide open. Most athletes begin training for their events weeks or sometimes months in advance. I wanted to start focusing on something. Putting a race on the calendar always made me focus and train better. Without a goal, it's easier to lose focus on anything we do in life.

Without a goal, it's easier to lose focus
on anything we do in life.

My first thought was to find a similar race closer to home. I read about a race in Michigan's Upper Peninsula, but I immediately ruled it out. I couldn't even finish reading the race description. It sounded so hard. Only a crazy person would do it! I began looking for other shorter races, but nothing jumped out at me. Nothing inside of me said, "I have to do that!"

I ended up deciding on a series of mid-length races in Michigan. Everything seemed to fit and they were close to home. Since they were not long races, I wouldn't have to put in as much training time. Also, many of my friends would be racing there. I like to laugh and have fun … a lot. So I was looking forward to racing with them. I knew we'd have a great time. There was just one problem. None of those races made me reach down inside and say, "I have to do that!" None of them got me that excited.

Training season got underway and things were going well. My strength was growing and my speed was increasing. I was content, except one little detail in the back of my mind kept bugging me. I had the feeling I should once again check the races that were within a day's drive. My thinking was maybe I had missed one. Maybe the "one" I was looking for was still out there. I had already searched every website and Facebook page of the known races up to this point. Nothing was a fit.

One morning, I was sitting at home and thought, "I'm going to give this one more try." I googled "mountain bike races in the Midwest." Nothing caught my attention as I scrolled through them, until I got to one. It was a race I had never fully read about because I couldn't get past the opening description: "100 miles of rugged single track, all uphill!" This time, I kept reading.

The race was relatively new and I couldn't find a lot of information about it. Their website said, "It's the hardest thing you'll ever do on a mountain bike, period!" Many races make that claim, but very few actually deliver on it. I could feel something inside of me immediately saying, "I have to do this!"

It was at this point I immediately went into self-examination mode. One side of me was saying, "What are you thinking? Are you some kind of nut? Only a truly sadistic person would want to put themselves through that kind of pure torture." Technical rugged single-track was my biggest weakness as a rider. This race was full of it from beginning to end—100 nonstop miles of it, to be exact. Let's not forget, all while riding uphill!

I knew in an instant my logical side had no chance in this decision. This was my race! Something had changed in me during the previous weeks. Something had grown as I let go of my Leadville dream. I didn't know what I was looking for. I just knew I would know it when I saw it. Long before this day, I had already made the decision to let go and let God guide my season. I prayed about it and didn't worry about what races to do. I wasn't expecting anything like this, though. Within a few days, I was signed up for this race.

Chasing Marji

The quest begins and her name is The Marji Gesick, a mountain bike race. Yes, the race is a "she" to me. I'm not exactly sure why we do this. My truck has a name, Michelle's car has a name, all my bikes have fun names: Maryanne, Ginger, and Rosemary. It always seems to be a female name, too. It's almost like we want to bring out the majesty, the queen-like traits of an inanimate object. Marji Gesick was the name of this mountain bike race and she was going to be unlike anything I would ever experience.

The immediate sense of regret, fear, and doubt didn't take long to set in after I signed up for the race. Those minor details took a back seat to the deep sense of adventure I had. I was refreshed with a new energy, a new focus. The goal-driven side of me was in full-on pursuit mode. I had set the destination. Now I needed to plot my course. I knew I couldn't do this on my own. I had limited knowledge about training, especially for something of this magnitude. I knew I needed to get the help of a seasoned professional who could guide me, someone who could show me how to train for an event like this.

I was refreshed with a new energy,
a new focus.

I enlisted the help of a friend. Jackie was a local triathlete coach who had done full Ironman competitions. She was a phenomenal coach. I knew I'd need her guidance if I wanted any chance to complete this beast. I told her what I was about to do and she agreed to help.

chapter seven

Training

Training Begins

With Jackie's help, I started slowly building the miles I needed to be prepared for the race's distance. She had me gradually increase my time on my bike each week, along with other specific strength training to help my core and upper body endure the abuse the trail was sure to dish out. We started out with a few hours a week. Ultimately, my longest training week was about 14 hours. My longest training ride was almost eight hours of single track in one day.

Single-track riding means riding on trails just wide enough to get through. Up to this point, it was my greatest weakness. One of my biggest concerns was the thought of being able to handle that much technical single track for that long. This type of riding demands your full concentration at all times. One slip or wrong move and you could be off the trail and on the ground in a flash. Getting hurt out there would not be good. You would be a long way from medical assistance. The course winds through the backcountry near Marquette, Michigan. The wilderness there is very rugged and remote, making any chance of getting to an injured rider very difficult. I knew I needed to get better at this type of riding. It seemed I had to fight the trail every time I went out. It wasn't until I started to pray about it and apply my internal dialogue that I began to conquer this fear.

I gave God complete control over my sport; He is my head coach. I often talk to Him during my rides. I started asking Him to show or direct me to resources to help me with this part of my riding. Then I started to apply those techniques. Most importantly, I was very intentional about what I said to myself while trying to learn these skills. I call it internal dialogue, also known as self-talk. It's important as an athlete to be specific about what's going on in your mind during training or competition. I was aware of the fear, but I learned to redirect that focus to the outcome I want, not the outcome fear gives. It's very hard to do at first; it takes practice. I got more comfortable with it, and it became easier and more fun. Now it is absolutely my favorite type of riding.

The power of God in us, coupled with our ability to direct our intentions, is immense. It doesn't get talked about much, but it is a tremendous source of power that He gives us. With it, you can literally accomplish anything that you and He do together.

> The power of God in us,
> coupled with our ability
> to direct our intentions,
> is immense.

The Bible tells us how some of the dynamics of this power work. One of the systems that govern it is God's system of production on earth. This is a law that works much like the law of gravity. You can't see it, but it's always there and always in operation. It is referred to as seedtime and harvest (2 Corinthians 9:6). In short, what you plant is what you reap. The more you plant, the more you reap. This law applies to everything we do in life, and training for this race is no exception. If we want results, we have to plant the seeds. In this case, put the training time in to get them.

The Training Process

Spending this much time on the bike seemed to be a daunting task in and of itself. Other concerns I had: How am I going to fit this much riding in an already busy schedule? Am I going to get bored out of my mind after a few weeks? What if I ride so much that I never want to see a bike again? Is my 40-plus-year-old body going to be able to handle all of this?

I was certainly heading into uncharted waters. While my fears and concerns were big, the challenge of it all and my drive for adventure were overriding the worries. Long days on the bike were filled with audiobooks, podcasts, and music. It's amazing. When you love what you're doing, it doesn't really seem like work. I loved riding and I loved spending quiet time unplugged from the world. Most of all, I loved getting closer to God. Each ride was filled with the anticipation of where I would ride today, what I would see, and what He would teach me.

Monday through Friday was work. I would normally get 1- to 2-hour rides in before or after work. Sunday was generally reserved for church and family. On Sundays, I would ride early before church. That way the rest of the day was for the after-church potluck and family time. Saturday was my only real open day of the week. That's when I would do my long rides. Friday night was prep time. I would meticulously plan and have everything ready to go for the next morning. If you're going to spend a few hours on your bike, you have to be prepared. There was a process to getting ready for the next day's ride.

I started by having my clothes laid out: rain jacket, shoes, helmet, and tool kit. Then I would pack enough food and water. Lastly, I would pray about what audiobook, podcast, or music that God wanted me to listen to on the ride. He would always lead me to exactly what I needed to hear. Many times, I would be amazed at the accuracy and relevancy of His message to me. Some days His message would apply to what was happening at that very moment in my life. Then other times I wouldn't understand the message until days or weeks later. It's amazing how accurate and timely He is. As the weeks and months went by, I could gradually feel myself getting stronger physically and spiritually. The funny part was I thought I was training this whole time for the big race. In hindsight, He had me training for many other areas of life as well. His lessons became an ongoing theme in my life.

Ski Hill—Another 20 Feet

One of those lessons has resurfaced repeatedly in my life, and I was definitely going to need it in the Marji Gesick. I want to share a story with you about my very first acknowledged encounter with it.

A few years earlier, when I was new to mountain bike racing, I entered a race that was held at a ski resort. I wanted to know what I was in for, so before the race, I rode the course that circled the property surrounding the ski mountain. The terrain was really tough, especially for me as a beginner. Going to the starting line, I was getting mentally prepared, trying to calm my nerves, telling myself repeatedly, "You can do this." The first couple of years I raced, I would get so nervous at race starts that my only thought was, "Let's just get this over with so that I can make the fear go away!" I still get pre-race anxiety, but it's a calm, focused energy that I have since learned to control with purpose. I didn't know how to do that back then. I was already way out of my comfort zone, so any unexpected surprises made the anxiety that much worse. Yes, you are reading this correctly. I trained and paid to do this. No, I don't know what's wrong with me.

As I got to the starting line, I could see the race officials talking to each other, pointing straight up the ski hill and then pointing to us, the group of riders. As this continued for a few minutes, chatter began among the riders. One person said, "They're going to add a climb straight up the ski hill into the race." I laughed to myself, thinking that guy has no idea what he's talking about. No one could climb that thing. It's way too steep to even consider. Soon others were saying the same thing. Then word spread as other riders came up to join the starting line. Now my laughter grew into concern. Could this be happening? Were they really going to add that? Sure enough, one of the officials came over and announced that climb was being added to the race.

I was already mentally at my limit on what I thought I could handle. Now this! No way was this happening to me right now. My first thought was, "How do I get out of this? Can I fake being sick? Do I have some kind of mechanical problem I can claim?" It was too late. I was lined up at the starting line, the gun was going off within a couple of minutes, and there was no backing out now.

Once the race started, I settled into what I believed was a sustainable pace. I was riding pretty fast, but I kept thinking of the big ski hill, and conserving energy for it was weighing on my mind. I held back a little but not much because I figured I was going to have to walk the hill. This was a multi-lap race, so I knew I would climb it three times. On the first lap, I hit the bottom of the hill with as much speed as I could in hopes that momentum would propel me up part of it. That got me about a quarter of the way up. I didn't even try to climb beyond that. I just started pushing my bike up, stopping every few minutes to catch my breath and relieve the burning in my calves and shins. I didn't really look up or around much on that first lap. I just drudged on. After getting to the top, I realized I was still alive. The hill hadn't been the death of me. This climb was definitely not something I was looking forward to on lap two, but I just tried to put it out of my mind until I would face it again.

The trail riding on the second lap was much better. I was now settled into a frame of mind many athletes call "the zone." When I'm in the zone, it's almost as if things are happening in a state of slow motion. Breathing becomes regulated; my mind, body, and bike all react to the trail and my surroundings as one object on a single mission. All senses become magnified; everything becomes hypersensitive. In this state, reaction times are much quicker than in an ordinary state of mind. You can even hear individual bystanders' conversations. Things outside of your mind are happening faster than ever, but inside it's almost as if things are happening in slow motion. Unfortunately, I didn't know how to stay in the zone this early in my racing career. It would come and go randomly. I seemed to have very little control over it.

As I entered the base of the ski hill, the zone left me immediately and was again replaced with a pit of fear and intimidation. This time momentum didn't carry me up as far. I think in part because I mentally gave up conquering the hill before I even got there.

This climb was different, though. This time I looked up and around me. I noticed that there were a couple of people actually climbing this thing on their bikes. The ones I could see were super lean, young, muscular athletes who were in peak condition, except for one guy. There was one guy who was in moderate physical shape, not super lean, and was astoundingly much older than me, climbing straight up the hill on his bike without stopping. He started out behind me but slowly passed. I watched him climb the entire thing all the way to the top, never getting off his bike. I couldn't believe it. My first thought was, "How is this old guy who doesn't even look to be in that great of shape climb this thing when other younger, better athletes couldn't even begin to do so?" He had something they didn't. It wasn't physical strength or stamina. He simply knew how to focus. I watched him carefully. He dropped into his easiest gear and focused on one spot, never looking beyond about 20 feet in front of his tire. Most other racers would get to the bottom of the hill, start climbing, then look up and be overcome with the sheer intimidation of how far away the top was. This guy simply focused on going 20 feet, getting there and going another 20 feet. In his mind, he wasn't climbing a ski hill, just a bunch of little 20-footers that happened to all be in a row. I thought, "If that guy can do it, I may be able to as well."

I finished my walk up the hill on that lap and started my third and final lap. I was feeling good on this last lap, so I decided well in advance that no matter what, I was either climbing the hill the same way the old guy did or I was going to pass out from exhaustion trying. As I rounded the last corner, I could see the hill in front of me. However, it was different this time. Fear and intimidation were replaced with determination. Instead of focusing on getting as much speed as I could to climb, I transferred my focus to what was really important: getting into the right gear and, more importantly, the right mindset.

Picking a spot about 20 feet in front of my wheel, I focused on it and hit it. Then I picked another spot, then another, then another. Learning from watching the old guy climb in the previous lap, I knew I couldn't look around or up. I knew that would be the end. I had to just keep focusing on another 20 feet each time. After what seemed like an eternity, I could actually sense that I was getting near the top. I couldn't believe that I was still on my bike and not walking. Amazingly, I climbed the entire ski hill from top to bottom with no stops.

This was a lesson God would repeatedly put in my life, over and over. I am a major thinker and planner. I like to know what I am doing in advance before I wake up every day. I'm comfortable with structure, security, and certainty. God knows this about me. He also knows your strengths and weaknesses, too. You see, He isn't always interested in our success; He's interested in our character.

Sometimes this means confronting and learning to be okay with the uncomfortable. You don't need to love it or embrace it with open arms. We just need to let go of control and know God wants us to learn to lean into Him. We can't do this if we haven't yielded to Him. He wants us to learn to develop a relationship with Him, to trust Him no matter what the outcome appears to be. We can't do that if we plan so much that we don't leave room for Him.

He isn't always interested in our success;
He's interested in our character.

The message of 20 feet at a time simply means not worrying about the outcome or the best route to achieving something. Our job is to keep our focus on God and go 20 feet with Him. Once you get there, then you can focus on another 20 feet again. You can go anywhere you want, 20 feet at a time. Yes, there is a time for planning and leading, but often our time is best spent yielding and following.

My Secret Weapons

As you may know by now, my ultimate secret weapon is God. I lean on Him and rely on Him, His wisdom, His overwhelming sense of peace, and His guidance. However, there is one trait He instilled in me long ago that has given me an advantage over many situations in my life. That trait is patience, but probably not the use of patience that you're thinking of. As I mentioned earlier, we seem to live in an instant gratification society. We want what we want and we want it right now!

This very concept is unnatural as it applies to so many things. I think this is one of the biggest reasons many of us don't make it to the finish line in so many areas of our lives. We simply don't understand how things truly work. We just don't have the patience to see it out. The accomplishment of anything worthy—having better relationships, building a business, getting closer to God, overcoming an addiction, losing weight, you name it—is a process. In most cases, there are no shortcuts. Building anything over time requires patience. It requires us to build one step at a time.

The real world doesn't afford us the luxury of skipping most of the course and heading straight to the finish line. Those individuals who understand this can accomplish things in their lives that most others can't or won't. Those individuals who understand this AND have a relationship with God that allows Him to guide them can literally accomplish anything they do in life. It's only with the combination of the two that you can take things to a level you can't even dream of. I was about to find out just how heavily I would need to rely on those two things in the Marji. All the hours of training, gym work, and praying were about to be put to the test.

chapter eight

The Race

The Start

All those months of planning and preparation came down to one thing: race day. My mind and body were filled with a mixture of emotions, fear, excitement, anticipation, and so much more. My stomach was turning a little, as it often does at the start of a race. This one got me more so than normal. I was anxious and even borderline nauseous. It's amazing how we can feel so many conflicting emotions at once. The buildup to this day had taken months—hours and hours of training, sore muscles, Saturdays of being away from my family. It all had come to one focal point.

The day before the race, I called my coach for our pre-race pep talk and game plan. She gave me invaluable advice. Without this advice, I may not have made it to the halfway point the next day. She said, "When the gun goes off, many people will start out fast. Let them go! The adrenaline and the excitement of the race will cause them to go out too fast. Pace yourself and be patient. You will see most of those riders later in the race after they quit or you have passed them because they ran out of gas. Your training and preparation for this race has gone very well. Trust the training. Save your energy for the hardest part of the race, which is the last 15 miles. Let me say this again, whatever you do, don't go out too fast. Go slower than you think you need to." She said it again, "Go slower than you think you need to. Go slower than you think you need to."

The excitement of being in that environment always causes a rush of adrenaline, which in turn can help make hard efforts seem fairly easy. That's why many racers go out too fast. The effort they're putting out seems easy and they think they can hold that pace all day, but once you've left the starting line and settled into a pace, the adrenaline wears off. If you're not careful, you can end up burning too many matches too early. Burning matches is an endurance athlete's term. Think of it this way: You start a race with a book of matches—how many matches are in that book is determined by the fitness level you reached while training for the race. You only have so many matches. Once those are burned up, you have nothing left. That means minimal energy is left to get you through the race. You must use them sparingly. If you burn them unnecessarily, you may put yourself in a position to barely be able to turn the pedals. In some cases, it may mean you won't finish the race.

My mind raced as I walked to the staging area. It was surreal, being there looking at the starting line. Standing there as all the racers did their last-minute equipment checks and prep, I said a prayer. I asked God to keep me and the other riders safe. I asked Him to be with me during the race, to guide me, and see me through to the finish line. I would end up talking to Him quite a bit that day. I would need Him more than I could have imagined.

Le Mans Start

The organizers of this race truly have some sick and twisted individuals dreaming up ways to increase the torture factor for riders, including doing something called a Le Mans Start. No, we're not all lined up under a big sponsorship banner on our bikes like a bunch of racehorses, pawing and chomping at the bit in starting gates. This race is different. Somewhere entangled in the race director's twisted mind is also a good sense of humor.

Somewhere entangled in the race director's twisted mind is also a good sense of humor.

The race starts with our bikes lying on the ground. Imagine a few hundred Lycra-clad mountain bike racers standing under the start banner, lined up like they're going to start the Boston Marathon. Yes, you heard me right, we started with a half-mile trail run and then we had to come back around to a small field with hundreds of bikes laying everywhere. The hardest part was finding your bike in the mix.

The best part was the actual race start. It didn't start with the usual shooting of a gun. I looked at my watch and knew it just hit 7 a.m., the official start time. Where were the race officials? I didn't see anyone even trying to get our attention or direct the group in anyway. Just as that thought hit my mind, I began to hear some music playing. I looked up to see a guy standing on the bed of a pickup truck with an electric guitar and amplifier. He opened the race start with an awesome Jimi Hendrix-style version of the "Star Spangled Banner," followed immediately with fireworks to officially kick off the race.

Once the rockets launched, we were off. I realized I made my first mistake only five seconds into the race as the discomfort in my feet immediately set in. I was running on an uneven trail in mountain bike shoes. If you know anything about cycling shoes, they have a hard sole. There is no flex or give at all. It was basically like running through the woods in a pair of old wooden Dutch shoes. My initial thought was,

"This is a bad idea. I'm going to twist an ankle before I even get on my bike." I slowed my pace and was just careful with every step to be sure my ankles were straight and I was staying upright. When I got back around to the field where our bikes were, it looked different.

The people who had been standing around the start area had dispersed. They were my markers on where my bike was. After a few seconds—which seemed like an hour of slight panic while thinking my bike was stolen—I found it. Finally, I could get my backpack on and get riding. I was happy to get on the bike and get going. I blew through the crowd, almost hitting someone who walked in front of me. It was a cluster of bikes and people everywhere in the field. It felt like an accomplishment just getting through the run and all of that.

The First Section

As I rode through the first few miles of the race, all I could think about was what Coach Jackie said. Her words echoed in my head, "Go slower than you think you need to. Go slower than you think you need to." I felt strong and rested. I wanted to tear the pedals off the bike and take off fast, but I held back. The first section of the course was a fairly open cross-country ski trail. The terrain was rolling, so there were just enough elevation changes to make you work hard. Little did I know this would be some of the easiest riding. It wasn't long before we entered the first single track of the day. In the past, I was intimidated by this much narrower trail riding, but not now. I was ready for it, or so I thought. All summer had been filled with riding in the tightest, roughest trails I could find down state where I live.

This first section of single track had more elevation changes than the initial ski trail. It was tight and twisty but not too crazy. It was still fun. That fun ended quickly as we came into an area that was root filled. Roots can be a lot of work. They take extra work from your whole body to absorb the impact. You have no choice but to fight through. When they're wet, it's like trying to ride on a bumpy skating rink. These roots were wet. It was early in the morning and the night's dew was heavy on the ground. I had to be careful on each root so I could keep the bike upright. After a while, that level of strength and concentration can start to wear on you physically and mentally. As you become more fatigued, the chance of a crash goes up tenfold. I made it through the initial section and thought maybe these will go away and we'll get to some faster single track. At least that's what I kept naively hoping for. That never happened; the course seemed to get harder as it went on, throwing harder obstacles than roots at me.

Getting through an unsupported 100-mile backcountry race requires a lot of stuff. At a majority of races, you have periodic aid stations to refill water bottles and get more food. Most races have several plotted along the course. This way every rider knows exactly where every station is and what supplies it has to offer. Many races even have bike mechanics at those aid stations to limit the chance of a rider having a race-ending mechanical failure. This is not the case at Marji Gesick. This race is mostly self-supported. That means if you want it or you think you're going to need it, you carry it with you. That means everything, from layers of clothing, water, and food to all your potential mechanical gear. If you don't remember to bring toilet paper, well then, I guess you use whatever nature provides.

You must pack light. You don't want to carry unnecessary weight, but at the same time you need to be prepared in case of emergencies or a mechanical breakdown. Food, water, emergency tool kit for your bike, spare tubes, a chain link, and many more things.

I had been training hard physically for this race and was well prepared that way. However, my gear was another thing. I didn't want to carry all that weight in my backpack. I knew that would be too much weight on my lower back for that long of a race. I had to disburse the load on my bike. So, I opted for a few packs that attached to it. One was under my seat and another was on my top tube just in front of my handlebars.

I had it all planned perfectly. The gear under my seat included most of the mechanical stuff—an extra chain link, tire tube, tools, and stuff I didn't need to get to easily. My top tube bag was the most accessible pack. I could reach down, unzip it, and easily pull out a gel pack or some food to keep going. I had two water bottles on the frame of my bike and was wearing a large hydration-style backpack, which had the majority of my water and electrolytes in it. I was prepared and had tested this setup on several rides back home on my local trails. I was proud of this setup. It was well thought out. Everything was where it needed to be and in the right place. There was only one problem. I hadn't taken into consideration the terrain difference between Lower Michigan trails and the trails in this area. These trails were rough and had no natural flow to them. They made you work for every up and down of the course. The downhills were actually harder than the uphills on many sections. There were endless roots and rock gardens to ride through.

The gear I had so meticulously attached to my bike had never seen trails this rough. Every mile of trail brought the same rattling, shaking, and abuse that an entire day of riding would bring on my local trails. When riding there, I never had one issue with the packs loosening or falling off my bike frame. The terrain in this race was different. I couldn't have possibly duplicated or imagined how rough this was going to be. The packs would not stay on my bike. I stopped a few times to tighten them, but after several failed attempts, I knew I had to come up with another plan. It wasn't an option to ditch the gear or food. I was already down to carrying just the essentials. I had no choice but to lighten the frame packs by putting all the heavy stuff in my backpack. This was a last resort because now it meant that I had to carry the extra few pounds on my back.

I couldn't have possibly duplicated or imagined
how rough this was going to be.

This may not seem like much, but when you put the additional stress on your back and legs over a 100-mile course, it adds up fast. I was worried about the additional toll it would take, especially on my back. The fistfight with the terrain was tough enough. I didn't need to fatigue my body any faster than what the trail was already doing. After readjusting everything, I paused briefly and said a prayer. I told God, "This race is in Your hands. I trust You will take care of me." Then I left it at that. I didn't overthink it, just simply put it in God's hands. In the back of my mind, I was still a little worried about it, but sometimes you reach points in life where you have done all that you can. When there's nothing else you can do, that's when you have no choice but to turn things over to God. Those can be scary places in life, but they often turn out to be the most rewarding. I've always thought it's God's way to help us give up some control and let Him take the wheel for a while. At those times, we really learn to trust Him.

chapter nine

The Going Gets Tough

The Crash

Things seemed to be going pretty good after a couple of hours or so of hard riding. I don't mean me pedaling fast; I mean me using every muscle in my body to fight the trail to keep upright. By sticking to a moderate pace, I was able to ride without much fatigue at all. My legs seemed pretty fresh, but my core and upper body just hadn't seen this much work on my bike before. I could feel myself getting slightly tired there, but nothing too bad. That really helped me keep my pace in check. What was fatiguing was my mind. This required more concentration than I was used to for such a long time. Most of the other places I had ridden required concentration for a few minutes, then the trails always seemed to have fast and flowy sections where you could give your mind a rest. Marji had some sections like that, too, but they were few and far between. I was also feeling pretty good about just picking up my first token.

The race organizers put four buckets of tokens throughout the course in undisclosed locations. The buckets were hanging on trees along the trail. Each rider had to grab one token from each bucket. That way, someone couldn't shortcut the course and cheat. To qualify as a finisher, you had to show the officials you picked up all four tokens by the end of the race. The joy of getting that first one didn't last long.

I hadn't realized I was mentally fatiguing until it happened. It was a simple root-filled corner I would have cleared easily under any normal circumstances. I came into that section with some speed, hoping to kind of ride or skip along the top of them. There were just too many and they were too deep. Halfway through the gnarled chunks of roots, I went down. I crashed hard. When I hit the ground, my bike went one way, I went one way, and half of my gear went another direction.

It seemed to happen in slow motion. I saw the section and thought I could clear it, but when my front tire hit the root wall, it stopped me dead in my tracks. My first thought (while starting to fly through the air in slow motion) was, "I can save this. I'll just pull up real hard on the handlebars and land on my wheels." It's amazing how in a crisis situation we can think several clear and concise thoughts in a fraction of a second. As soon as that thought entered my mind, it was immediately followed by, "No, you can't!" A second later, I was lying on the ground tangled into what felt like a pretzel. All I could hear was the rider behind me say, "Whooaaa!! Are you all right, man?" He sounded just like Spicoli in the old movie *Fast Times at Ridgemont High*. I couldn't even reply to him at first because I was a little out of sorts. Then after several seconds, I said what any logical person would say, "Yeah, I'm good, man!" That seems to be the typical guy response when something like that happens.

Most of the mountain bike community is awesome. Everyone seems to help everyone. I could tell in his voice this guy would have definitely helped me if I had a serious injury. He slowed up to make sure I was okay. After I got to my feet and checked all my limbs to be sure they were still moving, I sent him on. I said, "Keep riding, man. I'll catch up after I check my bike." I never saw that guy again; I sure hope he made it to the finish line. There seems to be an unwritten rule in a race like this. Everyone helps everyone. There is little official support in this race. In some cases, you must rely on complete strangers. Sometimes you're the one helping; sometimes you're the one needing the help. At Marji, we don't race against each other; we're racing against ourselves. We are racing to cross the finish line and conquer this beast.

After I did the usual post-crash bodily assessment, everything seemed to be okay. Yes, you get used to occasional crashes if you're a mountain biker. Crashing is just part of the risk in the sport. I guess if I didn't like risk and wanted to always play it safe, I would have to learn to play video games or something instead. Ha, that would never happen.

After realizing I was okay, an instant thought of panic hit me. Is my bike okay? I had another one of those moments where several thoughts hit me in a fraction of a second. "What if it's not? I'm in the middle of nowhere. I don't even know how far I'd have to walk to find a road. I don't even know in which direction. Where are my GPS and water bottle? They're not on the bike. I need them both to keep going. What if my water bladder in my backpack ruptured? There's no way I'd be able to finish the race without that." Yes, my mind was in a frazzled state, but luckily, clarity set in after a few seconds.

The first order of business was checking to make sure my bike was rideable. After a thorough check, all was good there. No cracked rims, broken handlebars, flat tires, or major issues at all. There were a few minor adjustments to make, but nothing serious. Then it was on to finding my gear that was scattered up the trail. I found my GPS and water bottle, got those back on my bike. The GPS was a little muddy but working great! You had to have GPS in this race. It was one of the few items the race director strongly suggested you have. This course was in the backcountry. The trails were marked, but anything can happen. Careless people could take the markers down, and you might miss a turn by not seeing one. If so, you could get lost really fast. After getting everything back in order, I got on the bike and started off again. The very first thing I did was say a prayer of thanks to God for allowing me to be okay and continue. I also thanked Him for the gifts He gave me. I have always said, "It's not what happens to you in life, it's how you choose to react." Our reactions often determine the final outcome.

It's not what happens to you in life,
it's how you choose to react.

As with all crashes in our lives—failed relationships, financial problems, health issues, you name it—there are always gifts that come out of them, gifts we wouldn't receive without the crash. The first one was that I was able to keep racing. That was a huge gift to me. I was okay and so was my bike. Furthermore, I had only lost a few minutes of time. That was nothing in a race this long. Sometimes bad crashes can be a domino effect that leads to other issues, if you let them. Loss of confidence and too much time off the bike leads to cold, stiff legs and mechanical problems, which can sometimes be race ending.

The most important gift from this crash was getting a hard slap in the face by an old friend called "perspective." I wasn't back at home anymore, close to my truck where I could just head back out on the trail, or go to my house and rest. This trail and race didn't have my full respect until this moment. Anything can happen out here, and it can happen in an instant. It can be completely out of your control and can happen before you even know it. Your level of fitness and experience is important, but ultimately it's not what gets you through something like Marji. You must be mentally ready for a challenge like this. If you're the type of person who quits things at the first sign or two of struggle, then this would never be for you. Maybe that's why the DNF (Did Not Finish) rate was almost 70 percent that year. Yes, almost 70 percent of the riders who started didn't finish. In my opinion, many of those riders were physically fit. They simply didn't have what it takes to push on mentally when the going got tough, really tough. I honestly didn't know if I had it, either. Sometimes you must do something so hard there's no predicting the outcome. That's the only time you truly know if you have what it takes or not. I was about to find out firsthand in the coming miles of this race if I "had it or not."

The Pain Cave

As the miles rolled on, I could feel the fatigue slowly set in. I was very careful to keep a steady pace, not too slow and not too fast. Well, as best as I could anyway. The uphill climbs were hard, but some of the downhills were much harder. They were like riding down the roofline of a small building, and then landing on layers of stacked cars to make your way down to the bottom … except these weren't cars. They were boulders. Other downhill sections were littered with layers of roots coupled with softball- to basketball-size rocks everywhere. The landscape could change quickly. Some sections looked like an ageless forest that was beautifully majestic, almost like something you would see in a *Lord of the Rings* movie. Other sections were dark and rugged, very rugged.

Many of these trails were literally cut in with hand tools like a pickax and a shovel. There was very little flat trail. Everything was up and down all day long. The hardest part about it was there were no big sections where you could recover. In many races, there are long, uphill climbs followed by long descents, allowing for rest and recovery. There was some of that in Marji but very little. It was a 100-mile battle with the terrain, your body, and your mind. The odd part was that I felt right at home. I had visualized this day for months. Now it was finally here.

It's hard to really take it all in when you're in the middle of the race, but I certainly tried at many of the beautiful river crossings and high overlooks. At one point you're so high in elevation that you can see for miles out into Lake Superior, the grandest mother of all the Great Lakes. There was beauty to behold here, and I was so grateful to be in its presence. I have always said little prayers off and on as I ride. This day was no different. I was just grateful to be alive and be in God's presence in the majestic place that He created. As majestic as it was, there was also an ugly side.

About 40 miles or so in, I entered what I call "the pain cave." All endurance athletes know this dark place. It's a place where everything hurts and you mentally hit a wall. It can be anything from mild leg cramps to some so severe your only option is to lay on the side of the trail in pain, hoping they'll go away. Other times it is an upset stomach or dehydration. The list is endless. This is where your mind really begins to take ahold of you, if you let it. It's almost as if your mind goes into protection mode for your body. Little thoughts begin to creep in like, "I'm tired. My back hurts. I have how many miles to go?"

Here is where you must guard your self-talk. These little thoughts can lead to larger ones if you allow it to happen. You can't let them; you must kill them on the spot. If unchecked, those small, negative thoughts always lead to larger ones, such as "I can't do this, what was I thinking, I should just quit." Those are the thoughts that you must gain complete control of immediately at their onset. This is almost impossible to simulate in training. You can put in a lot of hard training miles, but nothing simulates the challenge of a long endurance race like doing one.

If unchecked, those small, negative thoughts
always lead to larger ones.

I had just enough experience to know these times do pass; things do get better. I had done a couple of 50-mile races in the past. That helped me know the lack of energy, sore legs, and tough times do pass. They almost always do. It's amazing what slowing down your pace and assessing what you really need will do for you. I've had races where I felt like death and didn't think I could go on, and then 20 minutes later I had a second wind that lasted the rest of the race. It's not so different in life. Hard times always pass.

We will all have many different seasons in our lives. Sometimes they're seasons of plenty and sometimes they're seasons of lack. The key is to always keep God first and do what you know you need to do. Pity parties just make things worse, a lot worse. When I got deep in the pain cave, that's when I would try to remember to pray. Sometimes I would remember right away and sometimes I wouldn't. It always helps me focus and get back on track. I also did what I knew I needed to do. In this race, it was slow down, get some food and/or electrolytes, and then give it time until some energy returned.

The pain cave is not a comfortable place to be. But, it's the only place to be if you want to do better. If you can get comfortable with being uncomfortable, that's where the growth happens and where real progress is made. It's also the only place that you may start to see small glimpses of what your true capabilities are and what you may be able to accomplish. You can't learn much about yourself if you're always comfortable. If you get better in one area of life by being uncomfortable, it will automatically raise your level of play in all other areas as well.

Getting Lost

As we passed the halfway point, we came to another area where the trail was a gnarled mess of more roots and rocks. Many of the sections were so steep I had to get off and walk my bike up. Throughout the race, some areas had me lifting my bike up to the next rock, and then climbing up so I could just repeat it again to keep going. I came through what seemed like a climb in the single track that never ended. Then it went downhill. All the climbing I had done was just going back down. That was okay. That's what this race is all about, up and down all day long. However, this downhill seemed a little too easy and it seemed like I was going down for too long.

I actually got some recovery on it, but something didn't quite seem right. Somehow I missed a trail marker and got off course. Up to this point, my GPS had notified me if I was off course, but for some reason it didn't this time. It didn't for a long time. When riding downhill like that, you can't take your eye off the trail. That meant my eye was off my GPS. I slowed up a little to look at it. That's when I noticed it was giving me mixed directions. At the same time, I realized I hadn't seen a trail marker in a long time. That's when it hit me. I think I'm lost. My mind went into instant panic mode. Where was I? How far off course was I? How do I find my way back?

Somehow, in my mentally fatigued state, I missed a trail marker. My GPS didn't catch it because I was so close to the right trail it didn't notify me that I was fully off course. I kept riding for a little longer, hoping I'd see a trail marker, but there were none to be found. This was a huge mistake.

I stopped right away and tried to gather my wits and figure out where I got off track. I knew I had been riding for at least 20 minutes since I saw the last marker. This is where your mind starts to play tricks on you. There was an immediate feeling of heavy frustration, and then the negative thoughts started to creep in. I thought, "If I'm 20 minutes off course, it's going to be no less than a 40-minute delay. What if I can't find my way back right away? This could be a 1- to 2-hour delay." That leads into the thought of, "If I'm that far off, I may not even finish the race now." The mental toll of mistakes can compound and grow out of control quickly, if you let it. You can't let this happen or you'll succumb to it. If you allow negative thoughts to grow, they'll take on a life of their own. Then you'll literally become a slave to them. I think this is how many people quit on things in life. Eventually anxiety or depression sets in and you don't even know where it came from. One little seed that grew—that's where it came from.

I didn't really have the cognitive ability to think clearly at this point. Mental and physical fatigue had fully set in long ago. However, I did know I had to take control of the situation. So, I relied on my training and let it take over—no, not my physical training, my spiritual training. I calmed myself and again put the race completely in God's hands. My prayer was short and to the point. I said, "Lord, you are in ultimate control here. Not me. Please help me focus and guide me back on course, Lord."

If you focus on the problem,
you're going to be stuck.
If you focus on God and
let the solution come to you,
you'll always be better off.

Because I was so fatigued, I knew I had to literally give Him all control. That meant my strong will and often-flawed logic had to take a back seat to His lead. I rode on slowly, trying to figure out what to do. Then I saw a few other riders off in the distance through the woods. I rode over to where they were and noticed it was a trail I climbed about an hour before. Oh no, my GPS was still confused and I didn't want to backtrack the whole thing. My logical mind wanted to play it safe and just back track up the same trail. But something didn't quite sit right with that. My good friend George says, "If you focus on the problem, you're going to be stuck. If you focus on God and let the solution come to you, you'll always be better off."

So, I just relaxed and said again, "Lord, What do I do?" I quickly felt a strong sense to not back track but to climb back up the long trail I had just come down. I knew just enough to listen to that voice. I'm so glad I did, even though I had to go up one of the longest climbs in the race twice. I found the trail at the top and was back on course. Yeah, I did lose about 40 minutes and was still really frustrated with that, but I was grateful to be back on track and heading down the trail again.

Dark and Alone

The next several miles were filled with more ups and downs. Nothing new there. I did hit some more open ATV-type trails. At first, I was excited because I thought this section might be open, wide, and fast. Yeah, that wasn't the case. As I got going on the trails, they were just as hard as the other sections of the race. Even though they were flat, there were huge ATV-tire ruts everywhere. It was almost easier to pedal through the grass and weeds along the edge to at least keep some type of momentum. Eventually I came to what was called The Wurst Aid Station.

This aid station was not officially part of the race. It was awesome and such a welcoming sight. I needed a mental boost, and it really lifted my spirits. There were a bunch of locals grilling bratwurst and making grilled cheese sandwiches. They were giving riders high fives and offering any help they could. I kept that stop short because I knew I still had to make up time for my getting lost debacle. I wanted one of those bratwursts so bad at this point. I'm pretty sure I started drooling at the smell of the food, but I knew that mixture would not sit well in my stomach at all. However, I kept the bratwurst in mind. I thought, "That's my little carrot. I'm going to have one of those as my reward when I cross the finish line."

The day continued and the sun would set soon. I finally made my way to the one and only official aid station. It was well over the 60-mile mark. My sons, Austin and Dylan, were waiting there for me. They had all my extra food and gear. There was a bathroom, too. Wahoo!! I was never so happy to see a port-a-potty in my life! Let's just say that my bike seat was starting to irritate my backside. I jumped in there and put on what cyclists could call a lifesaver: chamois cream. Basically, it's a cream that goes on your sit bones, where you sit on your bike seat. It literally saves your skin, especially on long races.

All was going well, except one thing: My GPS battery was running low. It was rechargeable, but it didn't have a replaceable battery. For some reason, I couldn't find my charger. Luckily, one of the volunteers had a compatible phone charger, which they were nice enough to let me use. What I didn't think about was waiting for it to charge. I couldn't leave without it, so I opted to let it charge for only 10 minutes. It was going to be dark soon, so I grabbed my GPS, bike's headlight, and resupplied my food and water. Then I was off for the next section of trail.

There were two major sections of trail left to conquer. I heard the last two sections of trail were some of the hardest the course was going to throw at us, especially the last 15 miles. The course came back to this aid station before I would eventually hit those dreaded last 15 miles. Shortly after getting into this area, I could start to see why this section had its own uniqueness about it. It was rough, rougher than some of the earlier trails. There was no shortage of climbs, either. None of them were long, but they came at you constantly with very little time in between for recovery.

At this point, I was so deep in the pain cave that I was numb to it. Many of these hills were too steep for me to ride up. I had no choice but to push my bike. This started to create a real problem. The more I walked up, the more the pain in my left knee flared up. I rode what I could to keep that pain to a minimum. Many of these short but steep downhills were just too advanced for me to even think about riding down. I hadn't seen this hard of terrain, let alone ever tried to ride down. This meant I ended up walking quite a few of the downhills in this section, too. At this point, daylight was fading fast. I soon found myself riding in complete darkness. The only illumination was from the moon and my bike headlight.

There's something so peaceful about riding single track in the dark. The fat tires from your bike make almost no sound when rolling through the forest. The only one of your senses you can really use is your sight. Even that is limited at night because you can only see the small area directly in front of you lit up by your bike light.

I'll admit that it was also a little scary. When it's this dark and quiet, you hear every little noise in the woods. Again, your mind starts to play tricks on you. I know there are bears in this area, but I didn't think about them until riding through this section. I had been in the dark in the wilderness many times before. I knew not to let those thoughts turn into fears; it can happen pretty easily. I just said another prayer and kept riding. I said, "Lord, I know you'll protect me and keep me safe. Keep me on course and help this hurting knee."

Besides, there were bigger things to worry about than bears. My GPS battery was getting dangerously low. I knew I didn't have too much farther to go until hitting the aid station again. That's where I'd resupply quickly and then head out for the crazy last 15 miles. A few miles before I hit that aid station, my GPS battery died. The trail was pretty clear through this section, so I wasn't worried about getting lost because I knew I was so close. The fear I did have was wondering how I would ever get through the last section without my GPS. This was a major concern.

A few years earlier, I had eye surgery. Since then, I don't see well in the dark. On top of that, I'm slightly color-blind. The combination of these two things literally made it impossible for me to see the trail markers.

I could look right at them 20 feet away and would not see them in the low light. The only way I could see them was if my bike light was shining directly on them. That wasn't an option because the area my light lit up was too small. It wouldn't allow me to be able to see them. Frustration and slight depression set in. My mind went quickly to that dark place again. I didn't even give it permission to do that. It seemed to be my default mindset in this race.

Mental despair first, then the mental salvage work had to begin. After what seemed like a long time of panic, worry, and running multiple scenarios through my head of what I could do to finish, I finally remembered something very important. I hadn't talked to God about this problem. Just as I've done many times in my life, I thought I needed to solve everything on my own. This time I didn't have that option. This time I needed His help again, and in a big way. My prayer was short and simple. I've always thought there's no reason to get into big, long, drawn-out prayers. God already knows what we need anyway. I said, "Lord, you know my situation. You know I can't possibly finish this race without Your help. Again, I'm putting this whole race into Your hands. Please guide me to finish in whatever way You see fit. I would love it if You would miraculously and spontaneously charge my GPS battery to 100 percent." I have to admit I did keep looking at it over the next few minutes, hoping a miracle would occur. While God is still in the miracle business, He didn't choose to recharge my battery that night. He had something else in mind.

chapter ten

Help From Unexpected Places

Needing Help

A little while later, I pulled into the same aid station. This was it; I had made it to the very last section of the race, only 15 more miles to go. The last 15 are notorious for being the toughest part of the entire trail. The area was littered with worn-out and defeated riders, most of whom already quit the race. They were just lying on the ground trying to get enough energy to load up and go home. I don't blame them; this thing had used all of us way beyond our limits. Thankfully, my spirits were renewed when I saw friends and family there waiting to resupply me. I couldn't imagine trying to do this all by myself without any support.

My body was definitely tired, but somehow mentally I felt pretty good. I think it's because I had already turned control of my race over to God, so at this point I was calm and focused. I resupplied my food and water and grabbed a light jacket. Even though it was September, it can get cold. The daytime temps are usually in the 70s to 80s, but it can quickly drop below freezing at night.

My resolve to finish the race was strong. I came this far, and having little to no way to navigate the rest of the course was just another obstacle of the day. There was no option of quitting. I knew better than to give that thought any life at all. Since I had made up my mind that I was finishing this race one way or another, the only plan I could think of was to just start riding and figure it out. If I stayed on the trail, all would be good and I would be finishing this beast tonight. I figured worst-case, I'll literally walk my bike through the course if I must. That would be the only way I would be able to see the trail markers to know I was on course. This was absolute last resort because that would mean very slow going, I'd have to stop and shine my light at trees every couple of minutes to try and see the course markers. It would've taken all night, but I would've eventually found my way to the finish line.

At this point, I didn't even try to charge my GPS because I knew it would take a long time to get enough charge to be able to finish. If you sit down and rest too long, you don't get back up. I couldn't possibly risk fighting that battle, so I chose to go without it. Besides, after my prayer, I had a strange sense of peace about the whole thing. Don't get me wrong, I was still worried and a little scared, but it seemed to be controlled and not debilitating.

Right before heading out and getting back on the course, another rider walked up to me. He looked tired and defeated, but there was a glimmer of strength and hope left in his face. He said, in a somewhat worn voice, "Hey, are you going back out on the course?" Without hesitation, I said, "Yup, I'm leaving right now." He said, "Can you wait for me? Maybe we can ride together and keep each other going. I just came in and I need about 10 minutes to get my stuff ready to go back out." I told him, "Sure thing. I'll wait."

That was a welcome invitation. It had been a dark, lonely ride the past couple of hours in the forest. Someone to help keep me awake and motivated was going to be a fresh change of pace.

After getting ready, he came back over and we headed out. Once we got riding, I found out his name was Cameron. He had done several long mountain-bike races, even a couple 100-milers. When he said that, I knew I was in good company. Cameron quickly admitted that this was by far way tougher than anything he'd ever done before. He also confessed that he was going to quit at the last aid station. His wife said, "You can't quit now. You're so close." That's when he looked over and saw me getting ready to leave. He thought, "If that guy's going, I'm going, too." Having someone to ride with always gives you that little extra push.

Besides, quitting this race comes with its own set of issues. Some of the immediate sense of physical pain is over, but another pain eventually sets in: one of regret and failure, one of self-doubt and personal defeat. Physical pain goes away relatively quickly, maybe hours or days later. However, the mental anguish can last weeks or months. Then there's the official way that you must let the race director know that you have quit. You don't go out with any grace at all. You text the word "quitter" and your race number to the race organizer. That simple act alone has kept many riders on the course when they had nothing left and there was no hope of continuing. In some cases, they just can't bring themselves to hit "send." You know someone is completely defeated if they have to text the "Q" word to let them know they're out of the race. Ouch! Talk about adding insult to injury or getting kicked while you're down.

That's one of the reasons I love this race so much. It forces you to dig deep in so many ways. You have to get out of your comfort zone, so far out that you find what you're really capable of. I believe that we are all individually created by God as masterpieces, His works of art. We often fall so far short of our true potential. I also truly believe that if you can finish an event like Marji, you can apply that same formula to anything in your life. You can literally do anything.

I believe that we are all individually
created by God as masterpieces,
His works of art.
We often fall so far short
of our true potential.

It's not because you are smarter than you were before the race or that you've gained sage-like wisdom during the race. No, it's none of that. It's one thing and one thing only: You believe that you can do it. That's all. Competing in an event like this gives you a small glimpse into what you're truly capable of. This would never be possible without the pain and failure that's required to push you to that place. It's kind of funny how the rest of life isn't very different in many ways.

As we got riding, I immediately realized that Cameron had cat-like eyes. He was picking out the trail markers 100 to 150 feet before we would even get to them. In that low light, I literally couldn't see them at all. I was so grateful and immediately thanked God. I said, "Lord, I can't believe You brought me a way to stay on course. This is amazing. Forget that GPS battery I asked You to charge earlier." This was way beyond the help I had hoped He would provide.

The Final Push

The first couple of miles weren't so bad. It was uphill but manageable. Then it dropped us into some sweet, fun, flowy stuff. I started thinking that this whole feared last 15 miles was just a marketing ploy or an overhyped way to get people to sign up for the race. Yeah, well that notion ended real fast. The trail went from a warm, fuzzy teddy bear to a snarling, hungry lion in a matter of a minute! We made the turn up one section that was so steep we were off our bikes, literally lifting them up, and then holding the brake to pull ourselves up with our bikes, all the way up the grade. Both of our bodies were already beyond any level of fatigue we could've ever imagined before this race. This section would've been next to impossible for me to climb seated, even with fresh legs. After that came more of the same. I think we literally walked one-third of the last 15 miles. It's hard to say because my brain doesn't recall the detail that clearly. I was in survival mode. At this point, the trail was just a mixture of a jagged, rocky, rooty mess that twisted back and forth and up and down. The downhills were not even close to being rideable for my skill level, and our legs just didn't have anything left to climb the short but steep grades. The worst part was how they kept coming at us one by one with very little flat trail for recovery in-between.

As we were riding, we could hear some commotion up the trail, people yelling in the woods, and a few lights shining. What was going on? We are in the absolute middle of nowhere. I could hear some urgency in their voices and thought something must be wrong. When we got to them, we realized a rider had crashed. It looked like he had taken a really hard fall trying to navigate down one of the car-sized boulder drops. He was obviously in a lot of pain but seemed to be doing okay overall. We stopped to make sure he was okay, and he was. We talked to his friend with him, offering to help in any way we could. Then he said something that made me laugh on and off the rest of the night. His actual words were, "The fuzz is on its way, man?"

Now, I know I was tired and thought, "Maybe I heard him wrong." But before I got a chance to say anything, he said it again. "It's all good, man. The fuzz is on its way." "The fuzz," I thought. I haven't heard anyone use that word in years. He didn't need the fuzz; he needed search and rescue. I think to him it was all the same. Either way, he had been able to make contact with the local police department somehow and they sent someone out. Thank God his cell phone worked in that spot. Without that, who knows what would've happened. I still don't know how they knew exactly where he was. First responders are an amazing group of people. Without them, he probably would've had to literally crawl several miles to the nearest road, wincing in pain the whole way.

Realizing there wasn't a thing we could do to help, we rode off. I said a quick prayer for him as we got going again. "Lord, help ease his pain and get help to him as quickly as you can." Within minutes, we could hear the medic's ATV trying to make its way through the woods. There was no way to even get close to him. We passed them walking toward us on the trail, carrying a big stretcher to get him back to the ATV. There was no way around it. They would have to grunt him out of the woods on that thing. And then, when he did get to the ATV, that rough ride out was going to bring on a whole new set of pain. Overall, I felt bad but wasn't too worried about him. If he made it that far, I knew he was tough.

That incident was a real wakeup call. It showed just how dangerous this place could be. We continued to battle our way through steep switchback up hills and the almost straight-down drops. We were both tired and exhausted, but we agreed that it was great to have each other's company. We could see a light shining through the woods off and on behind us. We knew it was another rider. We had been seeing it for quite some time. He or she was out here fighting the fight alone. Whoever this person was, they had my immediate and full respect. As the light slowly got closer, we could see it was a man, a large man. He eventually caught up to us and decided to ride with us for a while. His name was Jason and he turned out to be a great addition to our group. He wasn't from the area but he had ridden this part of the trail the day before. It seemed as if he knew every twist and turn in the trail. The only thing I could figure was that Jason must have a photographic memory.

I can't tell you how much it helped to have a personal navigator to see us through the last brutal section of the course. When he caught up to us, we still had a ways to go. So, we all decided, let's just take it one section at a time and go slow to keep from getting injured. We had said that much earlier, but after seeing the guy who crashed, we took our caution to another level.

At this point, we only had enough energy left to walk up most of the hills and try to ride on the flatter or easy downhill sections. We were riding, walking, talking, and climbing for what seemed like hours. It's almost as if your mind and body go into a zone, a zone that tunes out everything else in the world. Your movement becomes rhythmic. It probably would look a lot like three zombies trying to make their way through the woods with mountain bikes.

As we were talking, I noticed Cameron's voice change to one of concern. His answers to my questions seemed to be more delayed. He didn't say much at first, but then he uttered, "I think the battery in my light is dying." "Oh, great," I thought. The eyes we were relying on to keep us on course were soon going to be useless. I hadn't noticed his light dimming, but as soon as he said it, I could see he only had minutes left at the most. When I say it was dark out here, I'm talking pitch-black dark. If you have ever been in complete darkness, then you know there is absolutely no way to see. You can wave your hand right in front of your face and not see a thing. The night was that dark out here. There were no city lights or streetlights to cast shadows. You had to have a light, or you simply couldn't see in this forest.

Our initial thought was, "What do we do? How is he going to be able to see?" I offered him my light with the thought that his eyes were way better, but he refused. Then we both realized, how would I have seen to get out of there? Suddenly, inspiration struck! Cameron turned to Jason and said, "Hey, how much farther do we have to go? How many miles?"

I had been running my light on low and he knew it. It had two brighter levels, but the battery wears out very fast on the higher levels. We knew it had to last the entire ride. Jason said we really didn't have that much farther, maybe a little over an hour or so. I knew exactly how long my light would last on the high mode. I did some quick math in my head and realized that we could do this. If I put my light on high mode, it should be enough for both of us to see.

We tested it out for a few feet on the trail and it worked. Cameron said he could see well enough if he rode right behind my back wheel. So that's what we did. I made sure to stay close to him and never get too far ahead. When we came up to a corner, I would just slow down to be sure he could see, too. Sticking together as a team worked. He could see, using my light. Jason was right there to make sure we were both on course and safe. He would give us almost turn-by-turn directions right to the end. We made it to the top of Jasper Hill, which I knew was right near the finish line. We grabbed our fourth and last token from the bucket hanging on a tree and then headed down for the last few minutes of the ride.

The adventure started at 7 a.m. the previous day and ended 17 hours and 50 minutes later as we finally crossed the finish line at 1:50 a.m. It was awesome to see my kids waiting for me at the finish line. The first thing I did was give them a big hug and thank them. They drove my gear, food, and supplies to meet me several times throughout the race. There is no way I could have made it through the entire thing without their support. I also gave huge thanks to my new friends, Cameron and Jason.

After several rounds of high fives and some quick retelling of our war stories, I looked around to soak it all in. The finish line was pretty much a ghost town at almost 2 a.m. I did see a couple of friends who stuck around to see who would finish. Their smiling faces were a welcome sight after that many hours of riding. There was one thing on my mind: Man, was I hungry. My mind immediately went back to the bratwurst

I had been thinking about all day. At 2 a.m., there were none to be found. But to keep on track with how the day went, something better came along. Congress Pizza right across the street was still open. Let's just say after 18 hours of energy gels and PB&J sandwiches, that pizza was the best I've ever had, even to this day.

I'd like to say I crossed the finish line with a swell of emotions, arm raised, tears streaming down my face in victory while crowds cheered in adoration. It just didn't happen that way. At that time of night, there were only a handful of people left at the finish line. It was dark and quiet. Sometimes in real life, things play out differently than what you expect. I was definitely excited to be finished and get off my bike. In reality, I was physically and mentally too tired to take it all in and really be in the moment.

On my way to the truck to pack my bike up, I said a quick thanks to God. There was no need for some long, drawn-out prayer or any other words. He and I both knew what took place that day. We both knew there was nothing left to say. I was grateful beyond words and He already knew it. It was a quiet gratitude, one only known when it is experienced. Yes, I was grateful for the finish but more grateful for the relationship with Him.

Hidden Blessing

It turns out that getting lost earlier in the day is what may have saved my race. That unfortunate turn of events seemed like the worst thing possible and was the ultimate frustration at the time. If I hadn't been held up there, I may have never met Cameron. Sometimes the setback is the path. If I hadn't met Cameron, I have no idea how I would've finished without a GPS and my almost blind vision at night. In turn, Cameron ended up needing me to finish, too. He needed encouragement, motivation, and support to keep going. And in the last hour of the race, he needed to see from my light. It's interesting how he allowed me to see. Yet, in the end, I was able to give him sight. Often, God brings us a helper in the darkest of times.

Sometimes the setback is the path.

It also turned out that Jason was a gift from above as well. He was our guide through the toughest part of the race. We can't always do everything on our own. Often, we need the guidance and the security of knowing that we have someone who's been through it, someone who knows how to get us to the finish line. Don't be afraid to let others help when you need it. That's part of what we are all here for. Each of us has strengths and gifts we can use to help each other. I truly believe that's one of the greatest beauties in our gifts from God.

The Right Head Coach

The training and competing in this race were the first time in my life I truly involved God from beginning to end. As I said before, He is my head coach. The race surely wasn't without failures, crashes, or problems, but the end result was crossing the finish line. Even though God did his part, I still had to do mine. I still had to have the will to fight through all the obstacles to get there. If I had given up near the end, He would not have been able to come through 100 percent on His part. He carried me through when I couldn't go any farther. He gave me courage when I needed it. He brought me a companion and a guide when I couldn't do it on my own. He will do the same for you.

My question for you is: What is your Marji Gesick? Is it an illness, depression, a financial issue, a substance abuse issue or a relationship problem? Whatever it is, He will get you through it if you lean into Him, not away from Him. He will get you through it.

chapter eleven

Perspective

Grabbing a Wheel

The majority of my training rides were by myself, but I always love to ride with other people, too. One of my training partners is my friend Scott. We are somewhat close in speed level. He's a little faster than me when we do training rides, but he's a lot faster than me when we race. I knew his skills through the single track were unmatched. I have not ridden with a better rider than him in the tight, twisty stuff. I knew he would always beat me there, but why was he beating me so bad on the non-technical and gravel road races? I couldn't figure it out. Then one day I asked him, "How do you race so well? I know your fitness and skill level as an athlete, but you seem to race above it." He gave me a piece of advice that not only dramatically improved my race performance, but it dramatically improved my relationship with God. He said, "If you're not on someone's wheel, you're losing time. Let the other riders do the work for you. That way you have the energy to go hard when the group breaks up or when it's time to climb a hill or sprint."

It was like a light bulb went off in my head. I had always been really good at trying to do things on my own with no help. My thought was, "Just work harder, put more into it, get tougher." In cycling, you often see riders bunched up in a tight group. They can save as much as 30 percent of their energy by riding right on someone's back wheel. It's called "drafting." The interesting thing about it is, you can't be two wheel lengths behind them or more than a foot or so to the right or left. You have to be directly on their back wheel for this to work. There is always a risk in being that close to someone's wheel. If they go down, you go down. There's no time for reaction. But, if you learn to do it skillfully, the rewards far outweigh the risk.

As I started to add this skill to my quiver of race arrows, I couldn't help but think how important this concept is in the rest of my life, especially my relationship with God. I have found that every single time, without fail, when I stay on His wheel and in His draft, things always work out. The times when I drift from His protection and safety are the times I am left carrying the load myself. Those are the hardest and loneliest times. When I find myself beginning to struggle in any area of my life—stress, busyness, worry—I just remember to grab His wheel and get back in His draft. That means to get back in His presence, get in His word, and go to the truth.

Why Did God Allow That to Happen?

I can't tell you how many times in life I have said that, especially before I truly knew Jesus and had a relationship with Him. I just couldn't understand how a loving God could allow such misery in this world. I guess the first thing to understand is that He didn't create the world that way. He gave us (mankind) free will and the choice to be good or bad. He doesn't want a bunch of puppets on strings. He wants us to choose for ourselves. The good news and bad news in this is that all of our actions, good or bad, affect each other. That is why He created moral law to go along with this freedom. Moral law gives mankind a framework in which to live that promotes harmony, unity, and community.

Moral law gives mankind a framework
in which to live that promotes harmony,
unity, and community.

He gave us the Bible, and one of its purposes is to show His creation (mankind) the right way to live. It helps us by showing the contrast between good and evil, what's right and what's wrong. I believe we often get weirded out by this. And no one wants to be shown what they do is wrong. All of this seemed so distant to me. For many years, I felt so removed from it that I just couldn't relate to this complexity or wrap my mind around it.

Over the years, God has not given me one direct answer to this question, which I have asked Him so many times. He has allowed me to see it in small layers. Or, I guess you could say, 20 feet at a time. He has allowed me to see it on an even deeper level when I spend quiet time with Him.

The other day I was spending some alone time with Him before I rode my favorite trail. He put something on my heart that allowed me to see Him and the world in a deeper, more complete way. I was thinking of a young man who had died just two months earlier. His name was Cody Tuttle. Even though I didn't really know him, I seemed to have this strange connection with him. My wife and I are good friends with his parents, but that's not the connection. He was an adventurer, a mountain climber, traveler, filmmaker, paragliding pilot, and especially a humanitarian. He came to his death in a paragliding accident in California in 2019. My connection with him was as an adventurer, and I was always intrigued by his travels and conquests.

His parents would often fill us in on what Cody and his wife had been up to. I loved to hear stories of exploration and fearlessness. They motivated and inspired me. I guess I liked them so much because they were living how most of us want to but don't. They were living with a raw freedom and boldness that many of us have given up for safety and security. I can't explain it, but there's something magical about living in your true self, living out what God created you to do or be. I think that many of us don't ever fully step into our true roles in life because we're bridled by fear. Sometimes I can't help but think, "What if we could all live out the lives that God intended for us and lived them out, with Him and through Him, in sync and harmony with Him but doing the passion that we loved at the same time?" That is how He created us. That is how He wants us to live.

In my quiet time with God that day, my thoughts went to Cody and his family. I knew they were all still grief stricken. It had only been a short time since his passing. God then laid a message on my heart, not on the outside but several layers deep on the inside. The message was, "I'm bigger than even this." Our completeness as a person doesn't revolve around what we do, what our hobbies are, whom we love, or even our family. It revolves around one thing, our relationship with our Creator. That was the direct message He laid on my heart that morning. Now I've heard that said before, but I never understood it with so much depth until that morning.

We all have a certain level of brokenness in our lives. There is no exception to this. If your pride is telling you that you don't, then you're just lying to yourself. So many of us walk around with these broken pieces, looking for someone else (boyfriend, girlfriend, spouse) or something else (work, hobby, bad habits). We seem to look for those broken pieces that fit our broken pieces. We often think that those that fit together will make us whole. The truth is, they never will. He laid on my heart that morning to always keep Him as my rock and to stay on His wheel.

One of my favorite quotes:

"Keep the dream alive
with the King inside."
– Cody Tuttle, 1987-2019

The Wooden Ruler

Imagine for a minute that you have a big ruler in front of you, something like one of those foot-long wooden rulers. Now hold it in one hand and take the area that your thumb covers and just focus on that little section. It's probably about an inch long or so. This little section is just what we typically can see right now in our lives.

That represents our immediate past, today, and maybe what we see as our immediate future. The rest of the ruler is your entire lifespan. God sees the entire thing, not just the small section that you can see right now.

Now look up from the ruler and look around the room. Remember that you can only see that little inch-long-or-so spot, but God sees out beyond the ruler, way beyond our lifespans.

Now look out a window and find the farthest spot you can see. Remember, you can only see that little inch or so spot, but God sees out beyond the ruler, beyond the room you're in, and way beyond what you see outside. He is bigger than that. He is so much bigger and vaster than we can even imagine. Remember that when tragedy strikes, when things don't go your way, and when life is overwhelming. Lean into Him because He is much bigger than whatever your adversity is. Even though Cody's parents still deeply mourn the loss of their son, they know God is bigger than even that.

Now, let's take this a step further. Have you ever prayed for something or even someone over and over, but the answer to your prayer never seemed to come? Know this: Sometimes God places that answer a couple of inches down our rulers. The answers can come at a later time. He can also choose to place events or occurrences on our rulers to help others. Sometimes it's the other way around. We often can't see it until days, weeks, or even years later. His ways are not our ways. He sees the much bigger picture.

One of the greatest visible examples of this capacity in which God works is hindsight. I can look back on many times in my life when I prayed for something and I thought that God just wasn't listening. Then at some point later, I would see that He was listening and answering my prayer the whole time. The story of the Marji Gesick race is a great example. When I got lost, I prayed about it. I couldn't possibly see how it was a blessing until after the race when I realized that if that hadn't happened, I might not have met up with Cameron. If I didn't meet up with him, I may not have finished the race. That's just one example. I can name countless examples of that happening in my life over the years, and if you think about it, I bet you can, too.

Conclusion

Woven and Grafted

I can explain how my relationship with God has evolved, even how it has happened in detail—what events have occurred and what outcomes resulted. However, I simply can't find any words in speech or in writing to explain my relationship with a living God. It's almost as if He is a woven or grafted part of me with every fiber in my being, physical body, and spirit. In reality, it's the other way around. I am part of Him. It's a quiet but powerful sense of truth, wisdom, peace, love, and gentleness. It's also a sense of fairness and justness, one that operates from a position that we cannot often see or understand. His ways are not our ways.

Sometimes that makes it hard for us to connect with or understand Him. Often the lack of understanding leads us to become narrow in thought and even arrogant. We expect the God of the entire universe, the Creator of the earth and all living things to be at our disposal when we want or need Him, but all on our terms. I can't help but think, how is this not like a small child trying to direct her parents what to do with their time, resources, and lives? I don't know about you, but I don't want to be that child.

I hope this book has helped you see Him differently. Maybe it will also help you see yourself differently. Remember, you are an amazing creation, literally capable of accomplishing anything you want to do in this world. But this can only come to full maturity if you learn to lean into Him. Always keep that in mind and always keep Him in mind.

Bumpy Cake Ice Cream Pie

Many of my friends and family don't have a close personal relationship with God. Honestly, sometimes I just want to take a plug from my brain and plug it in them. I want them to experience the joy, peace, and kindness of Jesus. Sometimes I just wish they could see it. I just wish they wanted to see it. They have no idea of how good things can be.

A local restaurant has a dessert they make called bumpy cake ice cream pie. It's my absolute most favorite dessert in the world. The interesting thing is, it was created by accident. This restaurant is famous for their bumpy cake. One day, the owner accidentally dropped the cake upside down on the floor in its container. It was covered with cellophane, so it didn't spill or touch the ground. She couldn't serve it to customers, but it was still okay to eat, just a little smashed. Instead of throwing it out, she decided to experiment with it. She mixed it with vanilla ice cream and the result was amazing!

I remember the first time I had it. I didn't know anything this good existed. Once you've tasted a dessert that good, it sets the bar much higher for any other. When I eat it, it's delicious and amazing, but it only lasts as long as it takes me to devour my bowlful. For me, this isn't long. Maybe two minutes, tops. For my wife, it's a 15- to 20-minute taste fest. She says that she likes to savor the flavor. I do, too. I just savor faster.

What if we could taste something that stayed with us? What if there was something this good that could be tasted and enjoyed for eternity?

This is just a simple example of a food that I'm talking about. Having a taste of what a relationship with God is like cannot be compared to food. However, it can serve as an example of what a starting point can look like. I just had to try the pie to know that I loved it. Sometimes all we can do is just give things a try. If you're ready to take your relationship with God deeper, keep reading.

Measuring Physical and Spiritual Fitness

I don't know about you, but if I'm going to do something, I like to know I'm at least getting better at it. When I started riding my bike a lot more, I could see the progress. I had a sense of accomplishment, and it felt good. It's easy to measure our physical fitness. We can see an increase in the weights we lift, the speed in which we run or ride, but it's not always so easy to measure our spiritual fitness.

The Bible gives us some guidance so we can see how we are progressing in our relationship with Christ. Here are a few questions to ask yourself:

1. How well do you treat others, including friends, family, store clerks, other drivers, co-workers, neighbors, etc.?

2. How well do you handle unexpected life circumstances such as running late, auto breakdowns, illnesses, injuries, and general situations in which things don't go your way?

3. An even harder question: How do you spend your time and money? This is the true measure of where our hearts are.

What's the Next Step?

My hope is you have read something in this book that has made you think about having a deeper relationship with God. I also hope you will take action and do something about it. Real action, not just say you're going to do it like last year's New Year's resolutions. This is much more important than that. The next step? You need to go down the rabbit hole. Forget about what you think you may know. You need to pursue Him directly. Your focus should be solely on a relationship with Him and nothing else.

If you want to know how God thinks, look at Jesus' life. If you want to know what's important to God, look at Jesus' life. If you want to know God, look at Jesus' life.

If you want to know how God thinks,
look at Jesus' life.
If you want to know what's important to God,
look at Jesus' life.
If you want to know God,
look at Jesus' life.

God allows each of us to make a choice. We can choose our own path that will naturally be corrupted by evil as part of our inherent human nature, or we can choose to be connected to His will and grace, via the Holy Spirit after the forgiveness of our sins through Jesus.

If you already know God and have a relationship with Him, I want to challenge you to take it to the next level. If you aren't sure where you fit in with Him or have never had a relationship with Him, right now is the time to start. The first thing you'll want to do is sincerely and truly invite Him into your heart (Romans 10:9 NIV). *If you declare with your mouth, "Jesus is Lord," and believe in your heart that God raised Him from the dead, you will be saved.*

Say this prayer right now – "Dear God, I know I'm a sinner and I ask for your forgiveness. I believe Jesus Christ is your son. I believe He died for my sins and that you raised Him to life. I want to trust Him as my

Savior and follow Him as Lord, from this day forward. Guide my life and help me to do your will. I pray this in the name of Jesus. Amen."

If you just said that prayer and truly meant it from the bottom of your heart, congratulations, my friend. Today is the first day of the rest of your life, a new life, a vibrant one that will be filled with the truth, wisdom, love, peace, and the joy of having a relationship with Him. I recommend that you get a Bible and start reading God's word. Second, find a good church in your area that preaches from the Bible. Be sure it undeniably states that Jesus is the only way to God. The Bible says this: *"Jesus answered, 'I am the way and the truth and the life. No one comes to the Father except through me.'"* (John 14:6 NIV.)

Some modern churches have directed their main focus away from God's word and have put more emphasis on creating a feel-good or entertaining experience for you. Be careful anywhere that God's word is not the main emphasis.

The Arcor Challenge

Have you ever had a streak of reading your Bible consistently, and then stopped the habit for really no reason at all? Have you ever lost weight, only to gain it back later because you abandoned the eating habits that got you there? Simply put, our habits define us. That's why it is important for you to develop good habits. The good news is, no matter where you are in life, you don't need to change a lot. I have found that if you focus on just two main habits, many of the other areas of your life will eventually fall into the right places.

The first area is focusing on your relationship with God. I call that being spiritually fit. A spiritually fit person has a growing relationship with their Creator. This gives them the guidance, wisdom, peace, and contentment that He provides. They also have a much stronger sense of self-worth and value. In turn, this allows them to live a fuller, happier life, not only for themselves but also for their friends, family, and community.

A physically fit person leads to a better quality of life. They have more energy, feel better about themselves, and live a much more vibrant life overall. You can have the greatest relationship with God, but if you don't take care of yourself, you may not be around long enough to share that gift with others.

To help you along in your journey, I have come up with a challenge for you. This is designed to help you create good habits in those two areas of your life. It's called the Arcor Challenge. The only thing it will cost you is a small amount of time every day.

Here are the rules. You must do these two things every day for 40 days:

1. Spend 20 minutes/day in Bible reading and prayer time.

2. Spend 20 minutes/day in some type of physical fitness.

For your prayer and Bible time—I have taken many of the lessons I learned from my time spent with God while riding my bike. Those journal notes are in a 40-day reading plan for you. Each daily lesson is already equipped with Bible verses to help you take your relationship with God much deeper.

---

1. Spend 20 minutes/day in Bible reading and prayer time.

2. Spend 20 minutes/day in some type of physical fitness.

For your workout time—You can do anything you want. Some ideas include taking the dog for a walk, going for a run, playing a sport, going to the gym, or even going on a bike ride.

Don't think about this challenge as a Bible reading plan but more like a training plan—one that will help you get in physical shape but also help you develop better communication and, ultimately, a better relationship with your Creator.

To learn more or if you're ready to take the Arcor Challenge, go to ArcorFit.com.

A Sidenote About Writing This Book

This book project was done 20 feet at a time … literally. He has given me whispers and nudges, sometimes days apart, sometimes weeks or months apart. However, He has made those just significant enough for me to take note. Through prayer, He has directed me on how to piece it all together. As I write this, I still have no idea what I'll do with the book when it's completed. Honestly, up until a few months before finishing, I wasn't even sure this was going to make it to being a book. I was just patiently praying, reading His word, waiting, and listening. Oh, don't think I didn't veer off course trying to figure out what He wanted me to do. In my haste to do something, I got ahead of God plenty of times. What I've found is that waiting on His timing is critical.

> "God loves people. He's interested in people, he wants to help them in their present situation, and he wants to save their souls."
> – BILLY GRAHAM

Vast quantities of time and energy are often wasted on obsessive worrying or planning. There is a time to focus on the big picture with planning and preparing. The majority of our time is often better spent by taking action and just focusing on the next 20 feet. The next 20 feet may mean just looking at what's right in front of you today— who you're going to meet, what you're going to do, who you may be able to help, or who may reach out to help you. Don't worry about what could lie on the trail ahead. If you do that and stay in constant communication with Him, He will reveal His plans and steps for you in His timing. The right timing.

Acknowledgments

This book took a long time and a lot of prayer to come together. I would like to thank my wife, Michelle, and my four children, Dylan, Austin, Brooke, and Madison. Without your love and support, many of the crazy things I try to accomplish in life would be impossible and absolutely meaningless. I am grateful beyond words for all of you.

I'd also like to say a special thanks to Aubree Mayhew. Without your help, these ideas and journal notes may have stayed as just that, ideas and notes. Thank you for helping me put all of this together.

God has brought so many amazing people into my life. I can't possibly list them all, but you know who you are and that you are appreciated beyond measure.

Lastly, I'd like to dedicate this book to my late dog, Zephyr. He blessed this earth for over 16 years. He was with me while I lived out much of the story of this book. He was with me in times of tragedy and in times of triumph, never leaving my side and always happy and content. I needed that joy and contentment around me many times over the years. He passed away just weeks before I finished this book.

About the Author

 **Aaron Hulett** is married and has four adult children. He believes strongly in living out the message of this book and giving back to his community. He's done this by serving in many capacities in nonprofit work, most recently as Chairman of the Board for his area Chamber of Commerce. He is also very active in his church, currently serving as an Elder at Light of Christ Lutheran Church. He still works in the mortgage banking industry, a profession he has been a part of for well over 20 years. In his free time, he loves anything outdoors, especially mountain biking.

ARCORFIT

Do you want to improve two of the most important areas of your life?

ArcorFit focuses on helping you continually improve both your physical and spiritual fitness!

Learn more at **www.ArcorFit.com**

Get the study guide for
Another 20 Feet!

You can now download a FREE companion study guide to *Another 20 Feet*.
Visit **ArcorFit.com/StudyGuide**.

CPSIA information can be obtained
at www.ICGtesting.com
Printed in the USA
LVHW081623300520
657026LV00032B/789

9 780578 656861